Over The Brid

CW00347931

Over the Bridge

Mary Baker

FOR RUTH

Mary Baker

2001.

BREWIN
BOOKS

First published in August 2000 by
Brewin Books, Studley, Warwickshire

ISBN 1 85858 166 4

British Library Cataloguing in Publication

A catalogue record for this book is available
from the British Library

Typeset in Palatino and
made and printed in Great Britain by
SupaPrint (Redditch) Ltd
Redditch, Worcestershire.
Website: www.supaprint.com
E-mail: admin@supaprint.com

By the same author

Primrose Time –
A Cornish Childhood Remembered
1993

Go, litle book and wish to all
Flowers in the garden,
Meat in the hall,
A bin of wine, a spice of wit,
A house with lawns enclosing it,
A living river by the door and,
A nightingale in the sycamore!

R.L.S.

ILLUSTRATIONS

Photographs   Small books and objects by Ian Sabell
Saltash Royal Albert Bridge by courtesy of
Francis Frith Collection, Negative No. 22479

All other photographs   From Mary Baker's Family Album

Drawings   By Rosemary Jones

Acknowledgements

I could not possibly thank individually everyone who has shown interest and enthusiasm for this little book so I say it now to each one, please accept my happy gratitude.

Over the Bridge

I was quite interested when my father told me that he and I and mother would be going away from Lelant to live a long, long way away, in a place called Birmingham. At that time, 1916, he was Excise Officer, based at Hayle, in Cornwall, and to 'better himself', as the saying goes, he applied for and was accepted, as an Excise Officer based in Birmingham.

He told me that we should go by train over a wonderful bridge built by a very clever man called *Isambard Kingdom Brunel.* At six years of age I was too young to realise that this journey would be the beginning of something and the end of something, but I never forgot the bliss of those years at Lelant. We left in November, and when we had said 'Goodbye' to everyone we set off on what I was sure would prove to be a great adventure.

When we steamed over the river Tamar, father said, "Now we are on the bridge that I told you about. We shall soon be in Devon: we've left Cornwall behind. Look." So I looked, but it was more interesting to look down than back – down at the river, the big ships, the small boats and the little people.

Brunel's Railway Bridge over the Tamar.

The time was November 1916, I was six years old and looking forward to a long journey on the train to Christmastime with my grandmother Schofield in Newcastle under Lyme, to seeing aunts, uncles, cousins, and my grandmother Green in Cobridge, so there was no time to be thinking about Cornwall, but I had not left it behind. No, I took it with me.

Once over the bridge, we soon came into the big, busy, noisy station at Plymouth. Some people got out, some people got in, and a porter came into the compartment carrying a flat basket with a lid, and gave it to father saying, "Your luncheon basket, sir," and father gave him some money. I had never heard my father called "Sir" before and I liked the sound of it. The basket was neatly packed with nice things to eat, so we had a sort of picnic, but it wasn't our dinner.

The journey from Lelant to Newcastle was long and involved changing trains from *High Level* to *Low Level* (or the opposite way) at Wolverhampton. Because of the long journey and because it was winter time and because I was young, it had been decided that we should *break the journey* at Bristol and stay the night at St Vincent Rocks Hotel and it was there, at six o'clock in the evening, that we had our proper dinner, with two puddings!

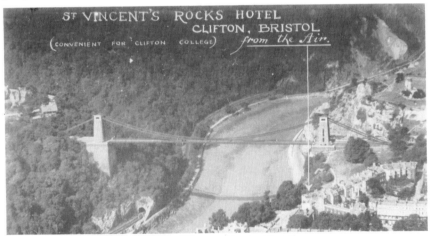

St. Vincent Rocks Hotel

I had to choose which one I liked best. The next morning after breakfast, we went to see another very famous bridge, and stepped on to it and father explained why it was called a "suspension" bridge and

2

Bristol Suspension Bridge

that it had been built by *Isambard Kingdom Brunel*, the engineer who had built the whole *Great Western Railway* as well as the other big bridge over the *Tamar!*

Father said that I must remember what he had told me, but to remember things in those days was so easy that I didn't even have to try. It is different in these days, but I am glad that I can still remember how pleased everybody was to see us when we reached Newcastle under Lyme at last and how interesting it all was. We stayed with Granny Schofield at number 11 Mount Pleasant, opposite to the big school, Newcastle High School for boys and there was outside the house, a footpath made of blue-grey bricks with a diamond shaped pattern on them. I had not seen any pavements like that – in fact I had seen very few pavements where I had come from and no bricks at all.

Newcastle High School

3

In Lelant the houses were built of big blocks of granite, with slates on the roofs, but here in Staffordshire the houses were built of red bricks with red tiles on the roofs, although the tiles were rather blackened by smoke from very fierce fires at Etruria, where pots and bowls and cups and saucers and plates were made. We had to go on the tram to visit my Granny Green at Waterloo Road in Cobridge, and going through Etruria in daytime was quite ordinary, but when we came back after tea, the whole sky glowed with fire.

These trips on the tram were very enjoyable to me, because in Cornwall I had only ever travelled on a train, except for when I once went in a sidecar made of wicker, like a long curved basket, attached to a motor-bicycle. A friend of father's drove this bicycle from Camborne to Lelant and we were all so interested in it that he asked if he might take me for a little ride, so I was tightly strapped in and we rattled away to St Ives, up the Stennack, round the back of Tren Crom and home. The trams rattled too but they were even more exciting than the motor bike, because when the driver stamped his foot on a certain iron pedal it made a very loud clanging noise to warn people that we were coming and to get out of the way. It had to be a loud noise so that it could be heard far off because someone driving a cart-horse with a laden dray needs time to get out of the way.

Horses had to be considered because the big ones with beards did all the lugging and tugging of heavy carts and vans, and the smaller ones took ladies for rides, or to do their shopping in pony traps or governess carts. No one in my family owned a horse, so when we were not going a long way, by the tram or the train, we had to walk.

Lelant had only three shops; Bennetts', Polglaze's and Sandow's and they all sold groceries and vegetables and sweets, but Newcastle had dozens of shops, which sold *absolutely everything* between them ,but separately. The grocery shops didn't sell vegetables, the shoe shops didn't sell clothes, and there was even one small shop near the market which sold nothing but clothes for babies. In the window sat a brown eyed baby doll dressed in toddler's clothes and I wanted it very much, for my very own, the next best thing to a real live baby. But I couldn't have it and had to make do with a very small celluloid baby doll which mother dressed in lace, gathered up and tied round with ribbon. It came from a shop which sold nothing but dolls and toys.

Nelson Place, Newcastle

To reach these wonderful shops we walked down Mount Pleasant, turned into Marsh Parade, where on the far side, there was a stall selling magazines and newspapers, and if it was the right day I had my "Rainbow" from there, and gave the money myself. Then we turned left past the swimming baths (which they had to have because there wasn't any sea to swim in) and into the Ironmarket and mother showed me the house where she had fallen out of a bedroom window when she was two years old. The doctor who was passing in his carriage, ran to see if she was hurt but she wasn't – he said that she was only frightened, and that her petticoats had broken her fall. I was glad nothing awful had happened to her, because I could not imagine having someone else for my mother if she had died.

If we walked on further, we came to the Guildhall, an important building, very sombre, like a giant's house. It stood in the street where the open air market was held on special days every week and Granny always went there on those days to buy her meat and butter and eggs and chickens and sometimes she bought a rather scraggy old fowl to make some tasty broth with pearl barley in it. Her butcher was a very fat man called *Cheseldine Cheadle,* and he wore a straw hat.

The market was teeming with people pushing each other and leaning over the stalls to see who had the best things to sell, and the farmers and the butchers were waving their arms and shouting that *they* had the best things, and it was very exciting, but once it got dark it was wild and wonderful. The stalls had upright posts at the corners and each stall had a kind of sheath hooked on to one of the posts and each stall-holder put a lighted torch into each sheath and flames and smoke flew out, dancing and waving, making everything and everyone look different.

One stall was piled up with cups and saucers and plates, and the man held a tray full of them as high as he could, calling loudly for people to make him an offer of money for the crockery and when no one answered quickly he said, "Right, you don't want it and I don't want it. So!" and he tilted the tray and let everything crash to the ground and smash to pieces and the people shouted, "Ooh!" as if they were frightened, but I think they liked it really because they stayed to see if he would do it again.

When it was time for us to go home the torches were still alight, all flaming and waving one way as if calling "Goodbye" to someone. But not to us because we went the other way, so that we could call at Swinnertons to buy cake for tea.

A child's life has to be a succession of "first times" spaced out, but for me a lot of "first times" came quickly, one after the other, some very nice and some rather tiresome, like having to be muffled up when I went out, in case I caught cold. I had five aunts, two with husbands and three without, and they all loved me very much and bought things for me. One gave me a velour hat with elastic to go under my chin and although it felt silky smooth and was very warm, I did not like it because it was pale pink, but I had to keep quiet and wear it. Another bought wool and knitted gloves for me and, although I can't remember who paid for them, it was decided that I must have a pair of gaiters because, they agreed, wisely nodding their heads, it was bound to get colder before long.

So we went to the shoe shop and I was fitted with leather gaiters. They were lined with woollen material, reached to well over my knees and had buttons and buttonholes all up the side, to be fastened with a button hook. These gaiters made me feel clumsy, and they creaked when I walked but the weather did get colder, as they had said it would and I saw icicles for the first time and wonderful crunchy sparkling snow, and suddenly one Sunday afternoon down came a shower of hailstones, like mothballs – not quite so big, but nearly - and it was lucky that it happened on a Sunday because father had come for the weekend from Birmingham. He said, "I know what to do," and asked Granny for eggs and sugar and some top off the milk and whisked it all together in an enamel basin. Then he scooped up a big bowl full of hailstones, put the basin in amongst them and stirred and stirred the mixture until it made a lovely ice cream, and we all had some, and it was the first time I ever had ice cream in winter.

I liked Granny's house very much. There was a fan-light over the front door and the floor of the hall was made of quarry tiles, red and blue, like the colours of houses and pavements. Granny washed the floor every week with soft soap and on those days the hall smelled especially clean. The door bell was high up, on a spiral fixed to the wall and when someone outside tugged the bell pull, the jangling rang and rang, for quite a long time.

The front room was called the parlour, and had lace curtains and velvet curtains and a big aspidistra on a small table in the bay window. The room was light and pretty, the piano had pleated pink satin at the front and had two brass candlesticks on hinges to illuminate the music. When someone played, the sound was not like the sound of father's piano, as I remembered dancing and singing to it when we lived in Lelant, and mother said it sounded like a *Tingalarum* and I couldn't say anything because I didn't know what a *Tingalarum* was, or what it sounded like, but she did.

The fireplace was very nice, with a lovely brass fender and fire irons all polished, but best of all was the mantelpiece, because of what was on it. In the middle was a gold clock under a glass dome. I don't think that it was *real gold* because my grandmother wasn't rich enough for such things, but it gleamed and I admired it. There were several small china vases, very dainty but best of all were the two big glass goblets coloured like the opals in mother's ring. They stood one on each end of the mantelpiece and each one had long pieces of thick clear glass dangling from the rim. I was told that these pieces of glass were cut in a special way and were called "prisms" and I found them magical because they could make ordinary light into rainbow light. I was not allowed to touch them, but that didn't matter at all – I could always sit and move my head to see the jewels sparkle out of them. This mantelpiece had something else which I had never seen before – a kind of pelmet made of silk brocade, with silk braid sewn on it in a fancy pattern and silken lace around the scalloped edge to finish it off.

Granny had made it. She and my grandfather met when they were both working for the same furnishing company in Newcastle, she as an upholstress and he as a French polisher and they fell in love and got married.

They must have been good at their crafts because they both did special work at Keele Hall. A member of the Tsar's family was exiled from Russia because he had married a young lady who was not to the Tsar's liking. She was not noble enough and they lived at Keele Hall from 1901 to 1910. My father said that the Grand Duke Michael brought his children to a social in the Victoria Hall, Hanley, and let them have slides on a tea tray slide which had been rigged up from the stage and that they all seemed very happy. It was a good thing if they were happy in England because they *were* Russians after all, but may be they made the best of it.

Mother's youngest sister lived near to Mount Pleasant, with her husband and their daughter Vera, who was a little younger than me. I liked having a cousin, and we played together and told stories and sang songs like "It's a Long Way to Tipperary", which was easy to learn because a lot of people were singing it and "Keep the Home Fires Burning" and "Pack up your Troubles in Your Old Kit Bag and Smile, Smile, Smile" and these songs made War seem a rather fine and cheerful thing to take part in, but I don't think it really was, because I overheard remarks when people didn't know I was listening. However, Vera and I accepted the way things were and enjoyed ourselves in spite of having to be "good little girls". At least we were not disobedient on purpose, but just by mistake, now and then, and people seemed to like us, so it didn't matter much, once we had been told, "not to do it again".

My mother's sister my Auntie Mary was a teacher and told us about the games played by the children in her class at school, like; "My mother says – " and we learned it and did the clapping, and "Johnny caught a fish alive – " for counting fingers. And she sang jingle songs to us, like:

"My name is Prickly Jack,
I've thorns all over my back.
When rolled in a ball, I care not at all.
For the cruel dog's attack."

Prickly Jack was a hedgehog, of course. Sometimes she sang grown-up songs at the piano just for fun and we sang those as well, whether we understood them or not. There was this one:

"Oh, oh, such a shame you know;
When she left the village she was shy.
But alas and alack, she came back;
With a naughty little twinkle in her eye!"

And this one:

"Lost, stolen or strayed;
A beautiful blue-eyed maid.
Last seen in Regent Street,
Long hair and tiny feet;
Dressed up like a queen,
Answers to the name of Maud;
Anyone bringing her home to her ma,
Will receive the above reward."

And this one:

"Joshua, Joshua,
Nicer than lemon squash you are"

And:

"When I marry Amelia, won't we have a spree!
Clocks with ruby faces, ebony dressing cases,
Hats we'll swop a-passing the time away."

These songs didn't seem to be about real people to me, but about people in funny stories, and the tunes were funny and laughing too, so we hopped and skipped about and sang and were happy. Our Granny was deaf and she could not hear us, so it made her sad, but not for very long because she was a smiling person. She made very nice toffee with vinegar in it, and kept the pieces in a tin on a shelf in the kitchen.

Christmas was coming and we were told that the geese were getting fat, and learned the rhyme about it, but for us the best part was

Christmas Eve, and Vera was allowed to come and sleep with me in the big double bed in the front bedroom. We decided to stay awake so that we could see Father Christmas, and when we heard the sound of someone's footsteps on the stairs, we fixed our eyes on the dim light coming through the half open door and could hardly breathe, but it wasn't Father Christmas who peeped in. No, it was Granny and I heard her whisper to mother in the hall, "The tinkers are still awake!" He *did* come, however, or somebody did, because there were nice things in our stockings and on the bed when we woke up, but we heard and saw nobody and it didn't matter at all, because it was lovely, lovely Christmas.

In Lelant mother used to put up paper chains from corner to corner of the sitting room at Christmas time, but here in Newcastle the only decoration was a Kissing Bunch, which Granny made of mistletoe and holly tied on to a small hoop with bright ribbons and hung in the hall. I liked the Kissing Bunch but I didn't like being kissed under it – in truth I didn't really like kisses at all and I wiped them off with my handkerchief or the back of my hand.

The Kissing Bunch was taken down on a special date, January *6th* and it not only meant that 1916 was over but that 1917 had begun. I knew that on the 24th of that month I should be *seven years old*.

My aunts at Cobridge asked me what I wanted Daddy to bring me from Birmingham for my birthday and I said, "A golden bracelet" and they said I must not depend on it because gold bracelets were very expensive, but I said that I was sure I knew I would get one, and I did and here it is.

My bracelet

Soon after my birthday we had to say "Goodbye" to everyone and travel by train to Birmingham and then to Harborne, where we stayed with Mr and Mrs Hewitt at 89 Park Hill Road. They had two children, Kenneth who was a little older than me and Margaret who was two years younger. Until the war was over Mr Hewitt wasn't there very often because he was in the army. It was very fine for me to live in the same house as two other children and it did not take long for us to get to know each other and tell stories and sing rhymes and have fun.

Margaret and Kenneth slept in the back bedroom and I slept in a camp bed alongside my parents' bed in the middle bedroom, and we invented an amusing game to play after we had been kissed "Goodnight". They came very, very quietly along the landing to my room and we took it in turns to smack each others' bottoms as hard as we could, hard enough to leave finger marks, if possible. Of course, eventually, one of us squealed as well as giggled because the smack was hard enough to hurt, and somebody came upstairs and told us to stop doing it and to get back into our beds but it didn't matter because I had to stop sleeping in that house very soon.

17, Wentworth Road, Harborne

My parents chose a house for themselves and me to live in. It was

11

number seventeen, Wentworth Road, just round the corner of Park Hill Road and as soon as our furniture came on the train from Cornwall we moved in and my parents did something rather unusual. Most people had square carpets in their sitting rooms, often what were called Turkish carpets, patterned in dark reds and blues with borders. What was left of the floor between the edge of the carpet and the skirting board, was stained with brown varnish. Our sitting room was different.

Mother and father and I went by bus to Chamberlain, King and Jones' carpet shop at Five Ways, and there they chose soft blue carpeting with a very small pattern and when a man had come and measured the room very carefully, other men came, bringing the blue carpet and laid it on top of some sort of felt, so that it covered the whole floor, and when people came they made remarks about it, because they liked it. The best thing about that house was the garden, because it had a *huge* oak tree at the bottom and in the Spring father made a wooden seat with holes at the corners and hung it on ropes over a very strong, low branch. It wasn't the kind of swing to go high in, like the ones at Queen's Park. It was the kind of swing to dangle in and think about things. I could look up and not even see the sky, that tree was so leafy and I loved it.

On the opposite side of the road, there were two schools. One was a very big one with iron railings, on the corner of Wentworth Road and Station Road. It had a playground with an open shed at the back and in the shed there was an iron trapeze and parallel bars. People as young as me could squeeze through the railings when the school gates were locked and we would run quietly round to the shed and take it in turns to turn somersaults on the bars, or to hang upside down on the trapeze – we called it "being a roasted turkey".

The other school was next door to the big one, in a double fronted house owned by Mrs Macready, and it was decided that Margaret Hewitt and I should go to that school. We went together hand in hand, along the side of the house and in at the garden door. The garden was quite big and had trees and shrubs on two sides and a high brick wall across the far end, opposite to the back of the house, but no flowers and no grass. It was all solid earth, trampled by children who for years had played games and run races on it. I was more nervous than Margaret, with good cause, because being seven years of age and not five, I was to be put in a class with boys and girls who had already been at school for two years and knew all about it, whereas I had never been to school at all. I could read and write and add up, on my fingers, and that was all.

We had three teachers, Miss Marshall, Miss Luckock and Miss Green. Mrs Macready herself sometimes read to us or told stories about her childhood in India. She wore skirts which nearly reached the ground and blouses with collars which nearly reached her ears, and she was kind to us. She was a grandmother but not quite so old as mine and three of her grandchildren were at the school and slept there. They were all called Osborne, but one of the girls had "Rosamund" as her Christian name. I had not known anyone called "Rosamund" before and I liked it, the sound of it and the colour of it and I wished that I had that rich name, but when I looked at myself in the mirror I could see plainly that I was a "Mary". There was no doubt about it. Whichever way I turned my face it was a "Mary" that looked back at me.

My classroom at school was upstairs, in what was intended to be a bedroom when the house was built but now it had no beds but desks, a blackboard, and a chair for whoever was teaching us, if she felt like sitting down. The two rows of desks reached from one side of the room to the other, close together and the back row was against the wall. This was a good thing for the people who sat in those desks, because we all stood up when we sang our morning hymn and said our tables but they had to stand on the seats of their desks, so the wall stopped them from falling over backwards.

The hymns we sang were not difficult "Ancient and Modern" ones, but hymns written especially for children like: "Jesus loves me, this I know for the Bible tells me so" and "There's a friend for little children" and "Jesus bids me shine with a pure clear light, like a little candle burning in the night."

They were easy to remember and to sing, but I felt rather guilty when I sang the last one, because it ended, "You in your small corner, and I in mine." I was prepared to try to shine like a little candle but not in a small corner, not even for Jesus.

"Saying" tables was more like singing, or chanting, because they went:

"Twice one ARE two,
Twice two ARE four,
And so on, through as many tables as we knew and learning a new

one when our teacher thought we knew the first ones well enough to get the answers right when she "dodged" and called out, "Mary, six fours?" and things like that, but not always to me, of course. We also had to learn how to spell six words from one day to the next, and the answers all had to come from "dodging" and we didn't like it very much. After that we had a lesson of something before playtime. Sometimes it was history and I didn't like the quarrelling and fighting and killing and dates:

"William the First 1066,
William the Second 1087,
Henry the First 11 hundred,
Stephen 1135"

I chanted these dates and remembered them, but I also chanted:

Nebuchadnezzar the King of the Jews
Sold his wife for a pair of old shoes,"

And:

"Oliver Cromwell lost a shoe
At the battle of Waterloo,"

And all these men seemed equally strangers to me, like people in very dull fairy tales. If history lessons had told me how my forebears lived, what they wore and ate and enjoyed and especially what women and children did, I might in time have come to like it better.

Reading and writing lessons were bearable and for some of the allotted time we were left alone.

Drawing was very dull, because we had to use rulers to draw squares and cubes and pyramids – to learn "perspective", I was told. Arithmetic was interesting, provided that it was not "Mental" and I was proud of the little ticks on my page of sums when I managed to get the answers right. The first time I had a grammar lesson I was absolutely baffled. Miss Luckock took the lesson, saying that we should be doing parsing and gave each one of us a sheet of paper ruled and noted like this:

Subject	Predicate	Object

Then she wrote in chalk on the blackboard several short sentences such as *Cat Eats Fish* and *Dogs Like Bones* and told us to write the words in the right columns. As I didn't know what "Subject, Predicate and Object" meant, it was a matter of luck whether I wrote the words in the right columns, unless I asked my neighbour what to put where. The others had done it before and were very glad to tell me ("she's never been to school before, you see") but we had to be careful because cheating was considered a misdeed, the sort of thing that "nice" children would never do.

Mid morning playtime was a very pleasant break from these lessons, and if the weather was fine we amused ourselves in the garden, sometimes playing games that we invented ourselves. We girls often skipped, using a long piece of clothes line held and swung by two people, one at each end. The rest of us waited to take turns and someone called out, "Run in," "Right leg," "Left leg," "Run out" and each one tried to skip as ordered without catching a foot in the rope. Sometimes the caller would shout, "Teddy Bear," and the skipping girl had to run in and do what the others chanted:-

"Teddy Bear, Teddy Bear,
Turn right round.
Teddy Bear, Teddy Bear,
Touch the ground.
Teddy Bear, Teddy Bear,
Show your foot,
Teddy Bear, Teddy Bear,
Sling your hook."

The boys never joined in the skipping, and very often played cricket at the far end of the garden, with stumps chalked on the wall. There was a sycamore tree at one side, and when it produced its sticky buds the boys chased us and tried to entangle them in our hair. But apart from that, they took very little notice of us, or we of them. When it rained or snowed we had to spend playtime indoors, either in our classrooms or in the hall, nibbling our biscuits if we were lucky enough to have any. One little girl knew of someone who worked at Cadbury's and could get cocoa-butter and her mother mixed it with cocoa and sugar in a saucepan to make a kind of chocolate which she poured into cocoa tin lids to set. When the chocolate was turned out it looked real because it had "Bournville Cocoa" on it, and it tasted nice too – a little bit powdery but it was a treat for us, because there were no sweets in the village shops.

How he knew when to go is a mystery, but occasionally my father would say, on a Saturday, "Let's go up to Bearwood for some sweets" and we would walk up Wentworth Road, along Crosbie Road and all the way up Lordswood Road to the Kings Head. It was a very pleasant walk between fields and once past "The Old House at Home" there was only one cottage on the left hand side, where the road dipped down, and then went up again to Bearwood where we found our little shop. Sweets were not rationed, but there were very few to be had and not every day either, so the shopkeeper would not sell more than a quarter of a pound to each purchaser. The sweets were not really very nice, but better than none at all.

Some of the food was not really very nice either. The only bread was not white and not brown, but an in-between kind called Standard Bread and I liked it, but when I found a piece of string in my slice of toast I didn't like it quite so much in case I found another piece. I never did, but I took small bites, even when I was hungry, to make sure that none was there. Meat was rationed and mother registered us with a butcher called Griggs, whose shop was in the High Street between Albany Road and the school end of Station Road. She had to stand in a queue often and by the time it was her turn to be served, there was nothing left but sausages, made mostly of bread, and rather dry. One Friday afternoon she waited and waited and found when she reached the counter that she had forgotten to put the ration cards in her bag. The butcher said, "You've tried that on before." She became so angry that he said, "All right, all right. You can have your rations" but she would not take anything and went home very upset. When father came home she told him all about it. She cried and I cried and father said, "Leave it to me. I'll go tomorrow and get something for Sunday dinner." So he did. And when he came back, mother said eagerly, "What did you get?" and he said, "Well – er – he only had sausages left" and they both laughed but rather ruefully.

Often when I crossed the road from school at midday for my dinner all that mother had to offer was boiled potatoes with gravy made of an Oxo cube dissolved in hot water, but she always managed to make a milk pudding – creamy rice, sago, or tapioca. Sometimes our Cornish friends sent us some butter by post and once they planned to give us a special treat. There was a knock on the door and I ran and mother followed, to find the postman holding in his two hands a shoe box wrapped in brown paper. Dark pink juice was dripping out of it, and the letter inside was dark pink and had to be dried before mother could read it. Our friends had filled the box with blackberries, the biggest and best, but when it reached Wentworth Road it was only three quarters full, because all the lovely juice had trickled away, and what fruit remained was very seedy. The postman was not pleased.

Once we had a very nice treat, but it didn't come by post. Father had a lightweight raincoat, which he often carried over his arm, but on this day he was wearing it when he came up from the train. All the buttons were fastened and his arms were folded under a bulge. When I asked what he had, he said that it was a secret and that no one else must know about it, just the three of us could know because it was a *whole leg of ham*, given to him as a present, not part of our rations, and that was why it was a secret. It was delicious and no part of it was wasted, because the bone made lovely tasting broth, much better than Oxo, when we had eaten all the meat.

At the first house round the corner in Park Hill Road someone ran a cookery school and at dinner times I used to scramble up the tall fence at the bottom of our garden to say, "hello" to the girls who were having a midday break. They didn't live there, but came every weekday to learn how to cook and looked like cooks already, in their long-sleeved white overalls. I did no cooking yet, except for rolling and cutting out left-over bits of pastry and making toast, by holding a slice of bread on a special fork in front of the fire, but I was allowed to iron a few handkerchiefs sometimes, after mother had made all the preparations and finished ironing shirts and blouses and petticoats herself. She had two flat irons which she heated on a low flame on one of the gas cooker boiling rings, and she ironed with one while the other was getting hot. She would hold the handle with a holder, like a kettle holder but thicker, and if the iron felt hot enough when she held it close to her cheek, she would use that one and set the other on the flame.

When we lived in Lelant father found small pieces of wax on the beach. He said it was Cordoba wax and seemed to value it very highly. One of these pieces, tied in a scrap of cotton material from the rag-bag, was rubbed lightly over the flat part of the hot iron to give a very smooth surface, and when the iron had been slid back and forth on a folded duster, the ironing could begin, providing that the cotton or linen articles to be ironed had been sprinkled with water and rolled up tightly beforehand. Woollen clothes had to be "pressed" through a damp cloth to make steam to drive the creases out, or the pleats in, and irons had to be very hot to do that. Mother also had a box iron, but I didn't use that yet, partly because it was big and heavy, but chiefly because the heat came from pieces of iron which were put into a glowing open fire until they were red hot. Each of these pieces of iron had a hole through it at the wide end so that it could be lifted out of the fire by a poker and slipped into the "box" part of iron. It was quite a risky procedure and I think that mother was right not to let me have anything to do with that type of smoothing iron.

On one side of us lived "the Marlows", a married couple with no children, and on the other side lived "the Griffithses", with a daughter, Molly, aged eleven and a son, aged eight months. When the weather was fine he sat in his pram in the front garden, and I looked at him and wondered whether I should get a baby brother or sister when I was eleven, like Molly. On Saturday mornings she did errands for her mother and when I was allowed to go with her, we were given twopence each and usually spent it at Bashfords, the baker's shop on the corner of Ravenhurst Road where it joins the High Street. They made very nice little cakes for two pence each and never minded how long we took to choose the ones we wanted. My errand was to take "the order" to our grocer at his shop next door to the Library and he would then have it all delivered to our house in a big basket on the front of a bicycle and mother would go round to the shop and pay for everything.

Bashfords was not the only baker's shop in Harborne village. There was Vickers' shop opposite to the Green Man public house, and Powells in the middle of the High Street, where they made lovely, sticky lemon buns and small buns, like scones, with sultanas in them, called "Farthing" buns because one penny bought four of them. Of course, they were *very* small.

I looked forward to being old enough to run errands myself, to go to the right shops and pay the right money for things. In Lelant there were the three shops, Polglaze's, Bennetts' and Sandow's, and a very small Post Office and no bakery at all – our bread was bought from Curnows at St Ives, but here in Harborne we not only had three bakeries but a whole long street full of shops on both sides!

We had our shoes from Mrs Baker, mother had a new coat from Mrs Kilby and Mrs Kilby's little girls came to my school so it was all very friendly.

Edith Powell came to my school too and Phyllis and Winifred Ince from the haberdasher's shop where mother bought all the things she needed for her sewing basket. Phyllis and Winifred lived over the shop with their parents and there as a staircase going up and a little window looking down, so that if they were all having their tea and the shop doorbell tinkled, Mr or Mrs Ince could come down and serve the customer.

Evelyn Corbett lived with her family over the fancy goods shop on the other side of the street and it seemed very pleasant to me, because there was always something to look at.

There was not much to look at in Wentworth Road, just children coming and going, sometimes a coal cart, the milkman with his horse and float and in the evening, the Post Office Mail van came very quietly down towards Station Road, and its trotting horse made a fine clopping noise that you could hear from a long way off. There were ten children living in the houses between Park Hill Road and Station Road and we played games together, sometimes in somebody's garden but usually on the pavement.

We played hopscotch and tig and I-spy and bowled hoops when it was the right time of year for hoops. Girls had wooden ones and drove them with wooden sticks, but boys had steel ones with handles attached, and they had to steer them rather than bowl them. We played with tops, not all the time but at the right time, and stuck them in the joints of the kerbstone while we wound the strings of the whips around them and then pulled very hard to make the tops spin and whipped and whipped to keep them spinning as long as possible. We made our own whips using a short stick and a piece of string with a knot in the end, and it was important to wind the string the *right* way round the top, unless you were left-handed, in which case you had to wind the string the *left* way round.

I can't remember how I learned the difference between right and left, but I remember very well the time when I didn't know it, because quite often I would – "- madly squeeze a right-hand foot into a left-handed shoe," like the knight in "Through the Looking Glass", but I never wept, as he did, because I did not know "an aged, aged man a-sitting on a gate". I just changed the shoes over until I knew which shoe went on which foot, without having to try them on first.

When it rained or snowed we played indoors. Someone would come to the door and say, "Can I play at your house today? Our Mom's on a line," or "Our Mom's got the headache." These Harborne children didn't call their mothers "Mammy" as I did when I first came from Cornwall and I soon stopped doing it, because it sounded babyish here. We played "Ludo", "Snakes and Ladders", "Tiddlywinks", Dominoes, "Draughts" and several different games with cards like "Snap", "Strip Jack Naked", "Clockface Patience", "Pelmanism" and "Happy Families". This last game had special picture cards to play with.

Everyone had a paint box, made of tin with little squares of hard paint and we all knew which colours to mix together in the lid of the box to make extra colours, but the best paint boxes had tubes of paint in them, with the names of the colours on the tubes. These names sounded really important, like *Vermilion, Cobalt, Gamboge* and *Indigo* and we used to go to Bradshaws in the village with our pocket money to buy any colour we felt we must have. I used to make butterflies by squeezing some blobs of paint on to strong paper, folding the paper through the middle of the blobs and then pressing outwards very hard and when the paper was unfolded, there was a butterfly, just needing whiskery feelers to be drawn at whichever end looked like its head.

Mother had a little magazine called "Home Notes" every week and once on the page for children, there was a drawing of a little girl with wings on her shoulders, flying straight up towards a cloud and underneath it said,

"Little girl,
Box of paints,
Sucks her brush,
Joins the saints."

And I remembered it and was careful. I worked hard at school and it did not worry me as much as it had done at first, although I still bit my nails. Reading began to be a pleasure, chiefly because there was so much to read about, and all so interesting. Every week I had the "Rainbow" and "Tiger Tim's Weekly". Mother had "Home Notes", father had "The Amateur Photographer" and a newspaper came through the letterbox every day. I was not supposed to read that, but I remember the front page of it, full of names in small print, with the headings saying *"Missing"* and *"Missing, believed killed"*. I tried to forget it because I didn't understand it.

On the opposite side of the road, next door to my school, there was a house which had been empty but now had some *Belgians* living in it. They couldn't speak English and had to live here because the Germans had driven them away from their own country. I didn't understand that either, and tried to make some sense of it by listening to what the grown ups said to each other when they thought that I was not able to hear them. Molly's father was a *Special Constable* that is to say a *"Wartime Policeman"* and he told my mother over the garden wall that when he had been on duty the night before, a German airship called a *Zeppelin* had flown over and that he had hidden under a hedge because he was so afraid of it, but apparently it just flew away. We children were more puzzled than frightened by it all and cheerfully sang, "Tipperary" or "Pack up Your Troubles" and a little song about sending Charlie Chaplin to the Dardanelles. We also chanted while we were skipping:

"Salute to the King,
And bow to the Queen,
And "that" to the German
Submarine!"

"That" was putting your thumb to your nose and we felt patriotic when we did it. Everybody loved Charlie Chaplin, and I went to the Picture House in Serpentine Road with my parents whenever one of his films was to be shown. There was a "First House" early after tea time, and a "Second House" which began soon after the First House people had gone home. The programmes were the same at each House, with News, an episode of a Serial and the Main Film, on Mondays, Tuesdays and Wednesdays, but on Thursdays, Fridays and Saturdays a different film and serial were shown and some people went to the pictures twice a week so that they could follow the serials. Children could go on Saturday mornings for two pence, and we very often went, several of us together. I would not have been allowed to go alone.

It was always rather draughty in the Picture House and it smelled of disinfectant but no one minded. One evening I was there with mother and the serial was called, "Madagascar Madness". I was frightened by it so mother told me not to look, and I knelt on the seat and watched the beams coming out of the oblong hole in the back wall, flickering through the cigarette smoke on their way to make moving pictures on the screen. Nowadays people talk of those pictures being "silent", and "black and white", but they were more grey and white really and were shown with someone playing a piano all the time. The films themselves were silent apart from some clicking but the Picture House was full of tunes, specially chosen to go with the picture on show and we could see the pianist in the corner low down at the front, because there was a little light over the open music book and it lit her hands and the keys as well.

I knew nothing about picture houses and theatres when I lived in Cornwall because there were none, but there were many theatres in Birmingham town, and one day we were taken from school by bus to the Prince of Wales Theatre in Broad Street to see "The Tempest".

We went in the early afternoon and sat near the front of the auditorium and were told to be very quiet except in the interval. All that I can remember of the play as then presented is a wild man called Caliban and one palm tree with a stalk like a very thick bamboo. Caliban climbed up the palm tree and it waved slowly from side to side because of his weight high up. We were told that Caliban was really a very famous actor called Sir Frank Benson but I didn't find that it helped me to understand the story of the play. I think that I was rather young for Shakespeare but my second visit to a theatre was to see a play for children at the Birmingham Repertory Theatre in Station Street. It was called "The Christmas Party" and I understood it and enjoyed it very much. Molly's aunt, Miss Phoebe Griffiths, taught at George Dixon's School in Edgbaston and she took Molly and me and several other children to see this play as a special Christmas treat. We had to go up flights of stairs to the back of the gallery, and then very steeply down to our seats at the front. When the curtains opened we saw three children in their beds not feeling well and sad because they could not go to a party. They had been looking forward to it, but their mother told them to go to sleep, so the lights went very low and when they brightened again there were Christmas decorations round their bedroom, and a trap door opened and a Christmas tree rose up, not a real tree but a cardboard one painted like a fir tree and decorated with tinsel. The children had a lovely dream party and we all went home happy.

Someone said that all the real fir trees were needed because it was wartime, but they didn't say what they were needed for, and I was not interested enough to ask. I should have been proud if my father had been a soldier in uniform, but it was decided that his work was *War Work* and he was given a badge which said so.

The Badge

My Aunt Mabel went to work in a munitions factory somewhere, and I heard people say that "munitions girls" made lots of money and bought fur coats but I don't think that she liked it at the factory, so she didn't stay long enough to get one and she was soon back home in Newcastle. I expect her little girl, my cousin Vera, was glad.

After Christmas 1917 we had quite a lot of snow and my lace up boots were treated with Dubbin to make them waterproof. I had several pairs of woollen gloves and when they got wet with snowballing I could run indoors and change them for a dry pair, but sliding was the best fun of all. We made a long slide in the middle of park Hill Road, just round the corner from my house, and all the children came to join in the sliding. It was exciting, and you had to be nimble because if you fell down people couldn't stop so they had to fall on top of you. It was not really dangerous because people didn't walk in the middle of the road and there was no traffic to speak of but one night someone put ashes and cinders on it. It was a pity because it was one of the few things that boys and girls enjoyed together.

Boys did not usually encourage us to join in their games, and if we asked if we could play cricket we were told that we could field but *not* bat. When the New Year came in it was time to think about going back to school, but I had something else to think about – *my birthday.* One thing about it I didn't like was the discovery that my birthstone was a

23

garnet. I wanted it to be an aquamarine or better still, a sapphire because they were both blue, like the sea. A garnet was the colour of tea.

We children were all very interested in colours and discussed our favourite ones, but I saw people's names in colour and also the days of the week – Monday, clear blue; Tuesday, creamy yellow; Wednesday, green; Thursday, purple; Friday, white; Saturday, pale gold and Sunday, very pale blue. The colours had nothing to do with the days themselves but everything to do with the sound of their names. Some music was coloured, some words were musical and there was so much to find out about that school seemed to use up very important time, but I had to go, and learn things that I really didn't want to know, like history, weights and measures and pounds, shillings and pence. However, in the afternoons our lessons were not quite so hard. We had drawing and painting, singing, reading and sewing, all tolerable, even pleasant sometimes. But sewing was so painful that it could have put us off it for ever.

The first thing we had to make was a doll's apron in white calico. It had to have a tuck in it, back-stitched with very small stitches to make it look as if it had been machined. Then the sides and the bottom edge had to be hemmed before the top edge was gathered tightly, "stroked" with a needle, loosened to the right width and set into a waist band. The calico was coarse and hard to push the needle through and sometimes it went with a jerk, right through and into my left hand, and sometimes I pushed so hard that the eye broke the skin of the finger of my right hand. I was told very kindly that I should wear a thimble so mother bought me a small one and I tried but it often fell off.

It took a very long time to make one of these aprons and then we had to make a doll's waist petticoat, also of calico. By the time both were finished we had tucked, hemmed, seamed by the "run and fell" method, made a buttonhole, and had sore fingers one afternoon a week for several terms. We were allowed to keep the little garments, but I thought that they were old fashioned, and they were rather grubby too, by that time.

Now that we had learnt to sew we were allowed to do some embroidery, so mother and I went down to Louie Warren's shop in the village to buy some Daisy Canvas and I chose Anchor silks in two colours to embroider my daisies on a tray cloth for mother. It didn't turn out to be a very beautiful tray cloth, but I was proud of it, and really enjoyed making it. Mother said she liked it too and bought a book for me with simple designs in it. She would always help me if I asked her, and taught me to knit properly with needles, not the kind of knitting on a cotton reel with nails in it, which we all did, but it only made a cord and I wanted to knit doll's clothes.

Little Girl's Fancy Work

It seemed to me that if I couldn't read properly I should never be able to do anything, so I tried to read as much as possible. Apart from a daily newspaper and the weekly papers delivered by the newsagent, there was a continuous supply of monthly magazines brought by father. A group of his colleagues at the Excise Office in Paradise Street made an arrangement to buy magazines, like "Pearsons", "The Strand", "Nash's", "The Windsor", "The Wide World" and "True Story", each person paying for one and keeping one, but everyone was able to read all of them because they were lent for a week, in turn.

We kept "The Windsor" and I did my best to understand the grown up world, from the little I could read, and the pictures in these periodicals. The advertisements were very interesting, especially those offering cures for all the unpleasant things that grown up people seemed to suffer. There were Carter's *"Little Liver Pills"*, Doan's *"Kidney and Backache Pills"*, Beecham's *"Sickness and Headache Powders"*, Dinneford's *"Magnesia"* to cure heartburn. One of these chemists made *"Bile Beans"* presumably to get rid of some of your bile if by chance you had too much. If you had a cold and a cough, there was Veno's *"Lightening Cough Cure"* and Owbridge's *"Lung Tonic"* and *"Friar's Balsam"* to put in a jug with boiling water so that you could breathe the spicy-smelling steam with a towel over your head. Some of the advertisements had little pictures like the one of a man sitting on a kitchen chair with his trousers rolled up and his feet in a bowl of hot water. Under the picture it said: *"Tiz for Tired Feet"* and there was another showing a gloomy little girl sitting on a woman's knee and the reading said, *"Mother! Is your Child Costive?"* and advised *"California Syrup of Figs"* to make the child quite well again. And there were *"Perry's Powders"* too so there was no need for children to be ill, except for things like measles and chickenpox which we were always told would be very good for us to catch when we were still quite young. I did not catch measles until I was seventeen years old and I wished that I had caught it when I was young because it was not at all nice at that age.

I couldn't always understand the stories in the magazines, but I tried hard to read them because there was such a lot to learn about, and lessons at school did not seem really interesting as a rule. All the same, we knew that we had to learn them and most became easier, and I didn't dread Mondays as much as I had done at first. Sometimes I heard people say "and as the day wore on" and I thought that may be days did "wear on" when you were grown up, but my days didn't. They were full of time and wonder. Mother came of a family of four sisters and two step-brothers and father was the youngest of seven children, four boys and three girls. When they talked about what they did and the games they played, I was envious because I was one alone, but I still liked to hear about it all and especially to hear their songs and jingles. Mother knew of lot of them like this:

"Little Tottie Brownshoes
Bought some half-a-crown shoes;
Oh, what a pity such a pretty little miss,
All through those half-crown shoes,
Little Tottie Brownshoes,
She's got a lame leg,
And walks like this"

Then she would go "dot and carry one", pretending to be lame, and we all did the same but of course I was getting to be rather old for that game so now we only played it when we had younger children visiting us.

Sometimes she sang little songs which were just funny, like this:

"I'm ninety-five, I'm ninety-five,
And to be single I'll contrive.
So that no man can say of me
That he hath made a fool of me!"

And this:

"Ha-hee, ha-hee,
He's waiting there for me,
He'll have to wait till half past eight,
Till white hair grows on a black man's pate,
Ha-hee, ha-hee, I'll make him wait for me,
'Cos if anybody knows a thing or two,
It's me, me, me, me, me!"

There was another interesting thing that mother could do, if she felt like it. She could remember many words which people in North Staffordshire liked to use and as well as I could recall, no one in Lelant used them, and certainly none of my school friends used them. For instance, if one of the boys got up to some mischief, she would say, "He's a little rappertag, that one," but if she spoke of a grown up rogue, daring but likeable, she would say, "He's a rumtyfizzer". What my friends and I called a "see-saw" she called a "queedle" and as well as "nowadays" she said "thenadays". And for "I keep my word", she said, "I stick to my tut". She *never* said "Give me your donny", instead of "hold my hand" as the Harborne mothers often did, and once when she said to one of them that the atmosphere felt "puthery" the Harborne mother said, "Yes, I think there's *tempest* about". I know now that it was good for me to hear all these different words and phrases, but at the time it passed over me like a shower of rain – and sank in.

In 1917 we didn't go away to the seaside for a holiday, and I told my friends that I didn't mind because I used to live by the seaside. They said, "Lucky thing" and I told them all that I could remember about Lelant and felt very proud and a little bit homesick. In 1918 it was decided that we should go to Borth in Wales for two weeks in the summer. We had a big travelling trunk made of strong wickerwork, lined with striped ticking and covered with what was called American cloth, black and shiny. The lid was arched, so it was good for riding on as if on a horse and especially good for slithering off. It had a wicker tray which rested on wooden bars across it, and mother packed dresses and blouses and shirts on that. In the very bottom she put our shoes and all our other clothes, including a whole set of winter underwear and outerwear for each of us, in case the weather turned cold, she said. It was strapped up tightly and locked, the van from the station came for it, but in a day or two it was brought back because it was too heavy, so mother had to unpack everything and take out some shoes from the very bottom and she was not at all pleased but this time it did not come back. It went off by the "C, D and D" method, which meant, *"Collect, Dispatch and Deliver"* and was waiting for us when we arrived at Borth.

We went by train from New Street and got there in plenty of time for father to take me to see the engine and wave to the driver, and he explained why the man with a very long handled hammer was hitting the wheels of the carriages. If a wheel was cracked the hitting of the hammer would make an unusual sound and if that happened the man would know what to do, but none of our wheels was cracked, so we climbed on to the train, somebody blew a loud whistle, waved a green flag, and we steamed away. I had to sit still in my corner and not touch the door handle or the leather strap which pulled the window up and down, but it didn't matter because it wasn't a very long journey to Borth and there were interesting things to see flying past us.

We stayed in *"Rooms"* and mother bought our food and the landlady cooked it. Borth was a very small place then, just one long road and we only had to cross the road and walk between the small houses on the opposite side and we were on the beach, where the sand was firm enough to play ball games on. I had a "first time" ride on a donkey along the road and back again and the days were bright and sunny all the time except for the day we went to Aberystwyth when it rained so much that I had to have a new pair of socks bought for me to travel back in but that was just one day in a fortnight, so no one complained and I got some new socks!

Once the holiday was over and we were home again, in spite of meeting old friends and telling each other where we had been and what we had done, it was very soon time to think about going back to school, and mother bought wool so that she could knit winter vests ready for me to wear when the weather turned cold. I did not dread school so much now – in fact I began to enjoy some of it, especially reading, and reading aloud, because some words sounded so right. For instance, if someone said "Galoshes" no one could help seeing big feet trudging through slush, whereas the word "Overshoes" meant the same as "Galoshes" but didn't make a picture when anyone said it. I was just beginning to feel the fanciful pleasure of words.

So, back to school, and September went by and October went by and November began but at the eleventh hour of the eleventh day of that eleventh month, there were some very loud bangs and we all became excited and some said, "It's the maroons" and some shouted, "The War's over," and some ran out into the road. Irene Inchley and her brother Aubrey lived near Queen's Park and she said, "They've built a big bonfire in the park, come and see it!" It was all so exciting that we didn't even put our coats on but ran and ran to the park and there it was, nearly as big as a house. Then Irene said that they had better go home and have their dinner before going back to school so I hurried home too, excited by the bonfire, and the war being over and everything, but mother was waiting for me at the garden gate and said, "Wherever have you been? Mrs Macready was very worried and came over to see if you were here, and you weren't and then I became very worried. Daddy is going to be vexed when he hears about this."

I began to cry and was so miserable that she said, "All right, I won't tell him but don't do it again – always tell somebody where you are going, or ask if you may go because we need to know." So I cheered up and told her all about the bonfire and how I longed to see it lit up and I did see it because after tea we walked up to the park, with people from everywhere joining us. There was a band playing, but when the bonfire flared up into the sky everyone shouted and cheered and drowned out the band.

And then the fireworks began. It was the most beautiful sight of my life and they saved the best till the last. A very big rocket flew up and with a crackling bang made the whole sky sparkle with stars and when the stars died away a wonderful thing happened. The whole sky was full of little tissue-paper parachutes floating and drifting pale against the dark sky. They seemed to come from nowhere and a lot of children seemed to come from nowhere too and ran about, hoping to catch one but the trees caught most, and we all went home, full of the excitement of it all. **The War was over!**

In November 1918 Margaret and I had been going to Miss Hall's Dancing Class in Moorpool Hall for about a year and we were very pleased when all her pupils were invited to Mr Lansdown's Christmas Party in December at the Plough and Harrow Hotel in Hagley Road. Everybody knew that very rich people lived in those houses in Hagley Road and that their children went to Mr Lansdown's class and our party dresses and petticoats were ironed and new hair ribbons bought and we hoped that we should look as if were a little bit rich too. We had our soft shiny dancing pumps to change into when we got there and it was all very exciting.

Near the end of the party we were asked to make a space in the middle of the ballroom because someone was going to dance for us. We had been dancing polkas and waltzes and valetas and things like that, but this was going to be Ballet. The music began quietly, and a dainty little girl in a pale blue tutu came tripping into the room and danced and I envied her and wished that I didn't have to be a *nobody*, sitting cross-legged on the floor. A lot of people crowded in and when she had finished her dance and was given much clapping, the little girl made her curtsies and would have gone back the way she had come, but the crowd at the doorway parted and a soldier in officer's uniform came into the room and someone told her to look and when she saw who was holding out his arms for her, she ran and everybody clapped and clapped.

He had come on leave from abroad and it was very exciting, like a story in a book. Soon after that our mothers came to take us home and we talked about it all the way.

Miss Hall didn't teach us how to dance ballet and when Miss Enid Bruton joined her we just learned the "positions" and no more, because the Foxtrot and the Onestep and the Twostep and the Tango were the latest dances, and even grown-ups began to go to dancing classes to learn how to do them, so Miss Hall and Miss Bruton taught us how to do them. No one was going to have polkas and galops at their parties any more.

When Auntie Mary came to stay she said that *Ragtime* was the latest music and sang about Alexander's Ragtime Band. I didn't like the new dances very much because they were all a kind of walking, but most parties ended with Sir Roger de Coverley and that was jolly and friendly and I liked it.

Most girls had a small party at home in the afternoon of their birthdays, and we wore our best dresses and took a little present and played games like "Pass the Parcel" and "Musical Chairs" until teatime when we were called into the dining room and told where to sit, around the dining table, which always had a fancy table cloth on it, sometimes with napkins to match. We always had jelly and blancmange to eat and home-made lemonade to drink and the iced birthday cake stood on a cake stand in the middle of the table, with candles on it. When we had sung, "Happy Birthday to You" and the candles were blown out, the cake was cut and anyone who didn't want to eat it there was given a slice wrapped in greaseproof paper to take home.

Then we played more games, like "Hunt the Thimble" and "Forfeits" which we played this way. If anybody did not obey the rules of a game she had to pay a forfeit and one girl was appointed to collect them. She would say, "Here comes the old woman from Botany Bay. What have you got to give her today?" It was normally a handkerchief, a bead necklace, a bangle or something like that. After a few games it was considered time to win the forfeits back and the old woman of Botany Bay would hold one of the articles up and say, "Here is a thing and a very pretty thing. Who is the owner of this very pretty thing?" The owner would say, "Me", then came the question, "Do you want it back?" and the answer, "Yes." And the old woman said, "Then you must dance a jig" or "Recite a poem" or "Tell a joke" or "Be a dog" or something and we all enjoyed people trying to do these things to win our forfeits back, and when we hoped to be lucky and not have to do something very silly or very difficult.

In 1917 father's friend, Joe Hind from Thorne in Yorkshire had come to visit. He was very interested in motorcars and while he was with us he went over to Erdington to meet a Mr Arthur Duckett who was making parts for motor cars in his factory. When Mr Hind went back home he gave me a *ten shilling note* and I was very pleased because it was the most money I had ever owned. Father suggested that I might like to help to win the war with it. I didn't really want to part with it but when I was told that I could go into a real *tank* to buy my War Savings Certificate, I agreed and we went to town, to Victoria Square where the tank stood alongside the Town Hall. We had to climb up an iron ladder to get into it and there I exchanged one piece of paper for another. Now that the war was over I decided that I would have my money back but the tank had gone and I had to exchange the pieces of paper at the Post Office, by Golby's furniture shop in Harborne High Street.

Mother gave me real money for my note – shillings and sixpences and a few pennies and half-pennies and I spent it very carefully indeed. There were sweets in the shops quite soon, most of them costing fourpence for a quarter of a pound and the shopkeeper had to weigh them on his scales but he didn't mind if someone like me asked for one ounce of Dewdrops and one ounce of Dolly Mixtures and he gave them to me in paper twisted into the shape of a cone. Mrs Cherry kept a sweet shop at the bottom of Park Hill Road and I usually called in there when I was taking and collecting father's stiff collars at the Mirror Laundry next door. He wore a clean collar every day and kept them in a papier-mache box made especially for stiff collars.

*Papier Maché box
for collars.*

Mrs Cherry sold sweets called "Ducks, Green Peas and New Potatoes". I never saw them in any other shop and as the "Ducks" were made of marzipan I spared the money to buy a quarter and got some of each, hard little boiled "Green Peas" and candy "Potatoes" dusted with cocoa and *two* "Ducks" if it was my lucky day. Sometimes when we had bought our sweets we went down a little path by the laundry to a stream and played there or crossed a narrow plank bridge into Thorneycroft's field. No one ever told us to go away and when the snow was deep Thorneycroft's was a wonderful field because it sloped and we all raced each other down on our home-made sledges.

There was just one thing to be careful about. If you came a little bit too fast it was pretty certain that the sled, with you on it, would shoot into the stream, so we usually rolled off, just in time and everybody shouted and squealed and it was wonderful fun, except for the "hot ache" when feeling began to come back into icy cold fingers. Some of us got chilblains, on our toes as well as on our fingers, bit it didn't stop us playing in the snow and being sorry when the thaw came.

However, there was always something else to do. My parents had spent their courting time walking all over the North Staffordshire countryside and as the country around Harborne was just as nice, they found some very pleasant walks for Saturday and Sunday afternoons. Sometimes we went through St Peter's churchyard, down the Hilly Fields, round the Golf Course and up the fields to Tom Knocker's Wood and back or sometimes along Lordswood Road, past "The Old Folks at Home" public house, then with fields all round, we would go to "The Kings Head", through Lightwoods Park, Warley Woods and come back to Lordswood Road by way of Beech Lanes. Father liked to give chocolate to mother, especially Swiss chocolate and we always had some to keep us going when we went on these walks, which were quite long for me. It might be Velma Suchard or Toblerone or Nimrod and this was my favourite because it had little bits of nut and honey in it like Toblerone but the chocolate was plain, not milk and I really liked it best.

We explored Edgbaston as well as Harborne, sometimes going to Five Ways on the number four bus and walking back along Harborne Road, or the other way round if mother wanted to buy things at Barrows' shop.

I always wanted to go down Broad Street as far as the Children's Hospital and to cross over to look in the Doll's Hospital. It was a small shop but there they sold everything for dolls and would mend broken dolls or thread new elastic into them if the original elastic had perished.

Some roads in Edgbaston were very pleasant with trees all the way and big houses, and when Margaret and I were allowed to go for walks together we looked at these houses and decided where we would live when we were married.

Hagley Road Tram

Hagley Road was a favourite road, not as quiet as some because there were trams going up and down to the King's Head but some of the people who lived in the lovely houses had motor cars and chauffeurs and nurses in smart uniforms, to take their babies out along the pavements in big Dunkley prams, some with blown up tyres!

Somerset Road was very leafy and peaceful. It led from the Green Man public house past the laundry belonging to the Bluecoat School where, so I was told, the orphan girls learned how to wash and iron clothes because they would probably be housemaids when they left the school and would need to know how to do it properly. The big house in the grounds on Harborne Hill was unoccupied except for a caretaker and the Bluecoat School itself was in town, near to St Philip's Cathedral, so the girls were only at the laundry on certain days, but when they were there, a lot of soapy smelling steam came out of the windows. All the houses in Somerset Road were old and big with lovely gardens but the best of all of them was on the far corner of Farquhar Road. It was called Whetstone, and where the lawns met the footpath, there was a stone with the name cut into it standing on the flat top of a very *low* wall. Along the Farquhar Road boundary there was a very *high* wall with the shapes of windows made in it and from a distance it looked as if they were the windows of a wonderful conservatory, because they were full of flowers and the colours glowed as if light was coming through them. But they were not real windows. No. They were stone frames for pictures made of tiles, making it the most beautiful garden wall I have ever seen.

Some people were beginning to build new houses where there was land available in these quite shady roads in Edgbaston and it was interesting to explore the half-built mansions. No one seemed to mind and one day when mother and father and I were looking round the ground floor of a house being built in Westfield Road, the owner of the house next door came round and asked father whether the house was being built for him and father said, "Oh no. Much as I would like it. I can't aspire to a house of this size." The man was a smiling grandfather kind of person and after he said politely that he was sorry not to be having us as neighbours, he invited us to go and see his garden. It was very big, full of all kinds of flowers in one part, with paths going through to another part full of fruit trees and vegetables.

He showed me a tall plant with a kind of flower at the top of the stem, and asked me if I knew what it was. I shook my head and he said, "It's a Jerusalem Artichoke but it doesn't come from Jerusalem. It's real name is Girasole because the flower turns round to face the sun all day, but when gardeners heard that word, they decided that it must mean Jerusalem, and so the plant got its name." He smiled down at me and said, "Learn something new every day and you will grow up to be a very clever girl." I said I would try to but really and truly I didn't have to try, because there were so many new things happening.

Father used to roam around the Jewellery Quarter whenever he had time, and one day he came home with something very interesting from there. It was a microscope, in a beautiful mahogany box with slots for everything to fit into. He set it up and we pulled out hairs from our heads and laughed to see them magnified so that they looked like pieces of string, but father joined the Microscopical Society and then he was able to borrow slides of wonderful things, some dead, some alive. The live ones were kept in slides like little glass boxes, flat and full of water. One of the creatures had a pretty name and was like a ball of fine hairs; it was spinning all the time and was called a Vorticella. Another one lived in a tube which he enlarged by making round bricks to build it up. Father put a very small drop of carmine in with him and he made pink bricks, then after a day or two he was given a spot of indigo and made blue bricks. I became very fond of that busy little creature and without the microscope I should never have known that such a thing existed.

Father borrowed slides of diatoms, minute fossils from the very bottom of the sea, each one like a priceless jewel, and he went off into the country with little screw top bottles in his pockets, to collect pond water in, and we examined drops of it, hoping to find something unusual and important, but I cannot recall anything except little blobs of jelly darting around. Father said that they were Amoeba and that they could divide themselves into two, and then into more and more, but they were really rather dull because they didn't seem able to do anything else.

Father liked Birmingham very much and wanted me to like it too so he took a lot of trouble to point things out to me especially when we were in town. I was impressed by the huge dark buildings around Victoria Square and when we went into the Excise Office in Paradise Street to meet father's colleagues, I was told that the roadway there was made of wooden blocks so that the noise of traffic would not spoil the concerts in the Town Hall but of course the traffic was of horses hooves on cobblestones in olden days. Nowadays motor cars were coming into use more and more, but father said that he was glad to be able to buy the worn out wooden blocks from the City Council very cheaply to burn on the fire but he didn't expect to be able to do it for much longer, because he was sure the road would soon be made of something called Tarmacadam.

He seemed to know everything and some things were more interesting than others, like the shop called Bucrel at the New Street end of Corporation Street on the right hand side. It was a toffee shop and on the counter, behind glass, was a kind of winding machine with two sets of arms and each arm had a small arm facing inwards. Somebody made the toffee in a back room and when it was cool enough to handle, he pulled it into a hank and draped it over the machine which he set in motion at just the right speed so that the arms, going opposite ways, stretched the toffee in a kind of figure of eight. This toffee was made in several different flavours, and raspberry was pink, lemon was yellow, coffee was brown, and as the arms went round, the colour became paler. Father said that was due to air being drawn in. When the toffee man decided that the time was right, he stopped the machine, cut the toffee free and eased it through very strong rollers which pressed it into little round sweets, covered with icing sugar to stop them sticking together. The shop was always full of people or so it seemed to me as I waited and watched.

Whoever took me always bought some of these special sweets for me and even the bags they were sold in were special too, because they were made of very strong paper and dangled from a silky cord threaded through with "Bucrel" printed in gold on the side, and I was proud when I had one to carry.

In 1919 our summer holiday promised to be very wonderful. We were to go, in July, to visit my aunt, uncle and cousins who lived on the island of Islay in the Lower Hebrides. I could hardly wait for the time to come, because I felt that it was going to be an adventure and so it proved to be, but two things happened which I could never have imagined or expected. This is how it all came about.

Our trunk was packed and sent on ahead, and we travelled by train to Glasgow, where we stayed overnight at a very big hotel at the station. The next morning we went in a taxicab to the Broomielaw, where we boarded our boat. It was cold and drizzling and the sea was rough and I felt sick and miserable but when we came ashore, Uncle

Charlie met us and said to me, "I've got just the thing to make you feel better," and he took a flat bottle out of his pocket and poured a small drink into the silver screw top lid and gave it to me saying, "Toss it off." So I did toss it off and it nearly choked me, it was so hot and fierce but someone gave me a toffee to take away the taste of it and I soon began to feel very warm, and eager to see Bowmore and meet my aunt and my cousins because I had never seen them before.

It was very exciting and they were all very pleased to see me. There was Margaret who was eighteen and quite grown up, and Jack who was fourteen and not at all grown up but between them was Tom and he was for me, the heart's desire. I had not really liked boys very much – they were rough, noisy and showed off and were bossy. When they said they were going to "have a swank" they never wanted girls to join in, but Tom wasn't like that. He was a manly boy and I had not met one before.

Main Street, Bowmore, Islay

He seemed to like me and I followed him everywhere as if I was his pet dog. He went to Allen Glenn's School in Glasgow and actually stayed there in "lodgings" during term time but now he was on holiday, at home, there every day and I loved him dearly. The family lived in a house which I found interesting and unusual. The sitting room or drawing room or parlour was upstairs and pleasant, with sash windows. The piano was there and when my aunt Dora was what she called "at home" friends of hers came and drank tea with her. Mother and I went up on one of those afternoons and father too, and when my aunt sang about the far Cuillins putting love on her, he played the piano and then someone asked me if I could sing. I said, "yes", and I sang, "The Lord is my Shepherd". It was all rather solemn, and I was glad when we had a cup of tea and a piece of cake and mother said that I could go now, if I liked, and I went downstairs, along the passage, through the back door and on to the beach. It's true. The doorstep was actually on the beach. There were no fences or hedges or gates, but sand and pebbles and shells and seaweed, and a boat. It was heavenly.

Myself with cousins Jack and Tom

In the dining room there was what looked like a very big cupboard but when the doors were opened there was only a wide shelf and that was my bed! It was unusual for me to sleep in a cupboard, but there was a window, and it looked on to the beach, and I was so happy that my thoughts were like feathers as I drifted into sleep. We were to stay in Bowmore for three weeks and it was decided that we should have a farewell picnic at Laggan on one of our last days and everything was prepared for it. We were all to go to this quiet beauty spot in McGibbon's brake. The brake was very like what I could remember seeing when I lived in Cornwall, but there it was called a wagonette. When it came to the house we all crowded round it and the horse shook his head and blew his nose and three steps were unfolded at the back so that we could climb up and take our seats along the sides. Then the baskets of food were handed up and off we went.

Laggan was a lovely little bay with white sand, some rocks and a patch of grass which the horse munched when he was freed from the shafts but before he had that pleasure he was driven back to Bowmore to bring to the picnic several people for whom there had been no room at the outset. One of them was Katie and everybody seemed to know her, except me.

She was thirteen years old, dainty and pretty, with softly curling hair, blue eyes and one foot held in tight bandages because she had sprained her ankle. "Lift her down, Tom", my aunt said, and as he lifted her and carried her in his arms, someone called out, "Is it over the doorstep, Tom?" and people said things like, "Who knows?" and "Maybe one of these days," and "Don't take any notice," and indeed Tom and Katie didn't, but I did. I felt fat, plain, a "little girl" with straight hair and I ran away to the sea, climbed on to the rocks and found a pool with anemones clinging to the sides of it. I knelt down, so that my shadow fell away from the pool, and I slid my hand slowly into the water until one finger touched one of the anemones open like a flower, and when those petals closed gently round my finger I was so overtaken by sadness that a tear nearly fell into the water, but I brushed it away because they were calling me and I went back to join the picknickers. Mother said, "You haven't been crying, have you?" and I said, "No, I just got some salt water in my eye," which was true but I didn't tell her why the salt water got there.

The next day all our belongings were collected and packed and the day after that we sailed away. The weather was mild, the sea was pale and calm and I looked at it. We stayed overnight at the hotel at Glasgow station and I went to bed early, sleeping in one of the two huge beds in the same bedroom as my parents. In the morning, I didn't want any breakfast and still felt miserable and hot so mother and father went out to see if either of them could find a chemist but it was a Sunday and Scottish Sundays were very much "closed shop" days. At last father found one who advised that I should stay in bed and be given soda water and a dose of "Gregory Powder". It tasted like nothing I had ever tasted before but I felt much better the next morning which must have been a relief to my parents because we were to travel home to Birmingham on that day. The guard on the train pulled the blinds down in the compartment because "the little girl" - me – was not very well and must lie down, but as soon as the train moved off we pulled up the blinds and I sat up and enjoyed the scenery and ate biscuits and drank some soda water.

The nearer we came to Birmingham the better I felt and I was longing to see my friends, so that I could tell them all about Scotland and Tom and being heart broken at the picnic, but when I woke the next morning, I had spots. Mother took me to Mr Shaw, the chemist, whose shop was on the corner of Albany Road and High Street, because I wasn't ill enough to go to Dr Middleton – in fact I was no longer ill at all. Mr Shaw that I had caught chickenpox about three weeks ago and that if I scratched the spots when they made scabs, I should have marks on my skin for ever. Mother bought something to stop the itching and I felt rather proud of myself but not so pleased to be told that I must not play with my friends until the scabs fell off by their own accord because until then I was contagious. I spent most of the days in the front bedroom with the window wide open and the friends came to the pavement outside, and we talked and played "I Spy" and things like that, so that the time passed until I was not contagious any more. I did not seem to be heartbroken any more either, because when we went back to school, Mrs Macready said that we were all going to be in an "entertainment" at the Moorpool Hall and that we should be dressing up, singing, dancing and play acting and that everybody would come and see us, so we had to begin rehearsals.

My class began to learn some French, like Je suis, "I am" and La pomme, "the apple" and some Latin, Mensa, "the table" but English was much better if you wanted to speak with somebody.

When we came home from Scotland I gathered that father did not always feel very well, because he had got Indigestion and when it didn't get any better, he decided to have a second opinion from a specialist who was the brother of one of his colleagues at the office. The second opinion was that he had a Duodenal Ulcer which must be removed by operation. These words sounded very serious and so I bought a small black china cat for ninepence at Corbetts for good luck and he took it with him to St Chad's Hospital in Hagley Road.

Lucky black cat

I was not told just how serious this operation would be and was not therefore surprised when I was told that I could go to see him because he was getting better. He was in a little bedroom at the side of the hospital, and could look at the trees, and at my cat on the window sill. H said that he was much better because he had been allowed a teaspoonful of water to drink but only if he would sip it and he had a funny little smile on his face as he said it. When he came home he was very, very thin and mother made him some dainty things to eat, like egg custard and junket and something called sweet bread, said to the very best food for a person who had been ill, but I didn't like it because it sounded as if it would be like tea-cake and it wasn't very sweet at all, but a pale kind of meat. However, he seemed to like it and got better slowly. I was glad that he was at home again because he was always doing interesting things. He could make a rabbit with a handkerchief and a church and steeple and a parson with his hands, and he knew all the different movements for playing "Five Stones", like "Cracks" and "No Cracks", "Lobster Pot", "Ones", "Twos", "Threes"

42

and "Fours" and lots more. He made up very good tongue twisters like "Sheep shriek" and "Shrimps shrink" and not many people could say them, not even grown up people, so children did not feel silly if they couldn't say them either, and everybody laughed.

Sometimes he made surprises like in the matter of the scooter. Just around the corner where Albany Road joins the High Street, next to the bank, there was a bicycle shop and in the window there was a scooter. Not a wooden one, but one made of metal, with rubber tyred wheels and I longed to have it. From time to time I mentioned it, to no one in particular, hoping that father would hear and take notice but when I said that it only cost a guinea, he said, "A lot of money" and went on reading. I went to look at it as often as I could and one Saturday afternoon, I said in a joking way, "That scooter is still not sold," and he said, "Then I think you had better go and buy it," and he gave me one pound and one shilling and told me to be careful and to come straight back. It was a very happy surprise and soon afterwards I had another surprise but this time, mother made it.

People were having their hair bobbed then – it was the latest style and I wanted my hair cut short and to wear a bow or ribbon on top instead of at the back.of my neck and I kept on asking mother, "Can I have my hair bobbed?" She would say, "No" in funny ways, like "Not now", or "We'll have to think about it" or "Daddy might not like it" or "Don't keep on about it". But I did keep on. One afternoon I came across from school and she was on the landing so I sat on the stairs and called moodily, "Can I have my hair bobbed?" and was amazed when she said, "Yes, but not until we have settled into the new house." I knew that we were moving and it was quite an exciting thing in itself without the hair bobbing and she seemed glad to surprise me and please me after saying "no" for so long.

The moving to a new house came about because our neighbours, the Marlows bought our house because two ladies, who lived at Tudor Cottage on Harborne Hill, bought theirs so we were to move into Tudor Cottage, the ladies were to come to the Marlows house and the Marlows were to move into our house. It all happened on one day in the Spring time. It was very interesting to move house and have a new address and a new garden, especially as this new garden had five pear trees, one fir tree, one copper beech tree and one laburnum tree in it, and the yard was good too, with a small stable, a coal house and a loo which we called the "outside WC" or the "lav in the yard". I was to have the front bedroom for my own. It had a little fireplace and was lit by a fan shaped gas jet, not very bright but a pretty pale blue colour.

Tudor Cottage, Harborne Hill

I was able to sail down Harborne Hill and round into Kingscote Road on my new scooter with no effort at all and climb the laburnum tree whenever I felt like it and the house had a cellar too, very dark and full of cobwebs, so it was altogether a very nice place to live, in spite of being much further away from school. Even that was pleasant sometimes, because on the way I could join up with Vivienne Shaw who lived on the corner of Gray's Road, or Doris Butler who lived in St John's Road and it was good to look in all the shop windows before turning into Albany Road.

The weather was warm and sunny and we girls decided to meet together on a Saturday afternoon and go for a picnic at Tom Knocker's Wood. It was exciting to decide what each one of us would take to eat, and I ran home for my dinner, thinking and planning, but father did not like the idea and said, "No, you may not go." I was disappointed and angry, thinking to myself, "Once again, it's not you." And I went back to school feeling sure that my friends would call me a baby but it turned out that not one of them was allowed to go! So we had to make the best of it and think of something else. One very good thing for me was to have my hair bobbed as mother had promised and we went to a hairdresser in Serpentine Road. He cut my hair, parted it on one side and tied the parted pair with a bow of ribbon. I was delighted and tried to see my reflection in all of the shop windows as we walked down the village, because I felt new. It would have been heavenly if it had begun to curl, but it didn't and I should never have been allowed a Marcel wave like some grown ups had even if I had wanted it but I didn't like the flatness of it so there was no argument. Grown up people liked it very much and paid to have it done with hot waving irons or did it themselves, and wore Kirbigrips and hairnets in bed to keep it in place. I heard them talking about it and was glad that I didn't have to look like that, or worry about it. Truly, I didn't have to worry about anything, it was a dancing time.

Margaret sometimes came to sleep at my house and we slept in the double bed in my bedroom. Very few motor cars and buses drove up and down Harborne Hill, but when one of them went by, a fan of pale light slid round the ceiling and we watched and talked about our future, where we would live, who we might marry and how many children we should like to have. As I was two years older, when Margaret asked, "But how do you get them?" she expected me to know but I didn't and had to admit it. I was much more interested in babies themselves than in the means of getting them and I liked the old-fashioned baby clothes, the long white gowns with tucks and lace and frills, the matinee jackets with ribbon threaded through and the veils made of net to keep dust away from the baby's face.

I didn't any longer hope for a baby brother or sister, but mother let me have a gown which she had made for me when I was newly born and I dressed my big doll in it. When babies could sit up, some mothers pinned little bows of bright coloured ribbon on to the shoulders of their jackets so that they should not become cross eyed, but I thought that it would look silly on a doll because doll's eyes couldn't cross. I had seen how they worked when the wig came off one of my dolls.

Some mothers dressed their babies in knitted clothes and there were patterns in "Home Notes" and "Woman's Weekly" to explain how to make them but I only liked knitted jackets and bonnets, sometimes made of *rabbit wool* as the fashion was or *Teazle wool*, which had to be fluffed up with a special wire brush. I worked very hard to make my dolls look right and mother helped me.

One day I was skipping in the yard and Molly, our neighbour from Wentworth Road came to see how we were getting on and said, quite casually, "The Marlows have cut down that oak tree in your garden." I said, "No" very quietly because I could hardly breathe. It was my first encounter with death and when I went to bed I let my mind dwell on it and wept until my pillow was damp. I could not forgive the Marlows for killing my tree when I loved it so much, and when I thought of it crashing down, lying still, waiting to be sawn up into logs, I could not hold the tears back and for several nights I cried myself to sleep.

I felt like a person in a sad story and when grief at the death of my tree began to soften, I tried to think of another sadness to cry about but it wasn't easy. I tried to imagine what it would feel like if I discovered that I was not my parents' own child but that they had bought me from the gypsies. However interesting that idea was, I did not shed tears over it because I could not believe it. I just did not look like a gypsy's child and I had something good to dream about instead – we were going to Cornwall for our summer holiday! Father bought an expensive new camera and Mother and I went off to Lewis's and I chose three different ginghams for her to make into new dresses for me, because I had outgrown my last year's frocks, even though they had been let down, and she wanted me to look nice because we should meet people who could remember us and they would be sure to "make remarks". It seemed long to wait for the day but at last it came and we

46

climbed into the train at Snow Hill Station and made ourselves very comfortable because we should be there until we reached St Erth. It was good to see the sea at Teignmouth and wave to people on the beach but once over Brunel's bridge there were the names. There were places in Harborne and Birmingham with interesting names, like Lordswood Road, Princes Corner, Ladywood, Queen's Park, Earlswood, King's Heath and King's Norton, so that it felt as if we lived where very grand people had once lived, but Cornwall was different. Wales had some places with unusual names rather hard to pronounce properly, but that was to be expected because Welsh people spoke a foreign language as well as English and their place names were foreign. Cornish places sounded mysterious and faraway but not foreign.

On one side of the compartment there was a map set into the pannelling above the seat and it showed the railway line from Plymouth to Penzance. Now that I could read, I found every station that we stopped at or passed through and called these names out with increasing pleasure and excitement, not only because I could see that we were on our way to where I longed to be, but because of the sound and the colour of these names.

The beach at Lelant

When we reached a wonderful viaduct and father told me to look down because we were above the tree tops, it was not the greenery or the granite which impressed me but the word, *Menheniot*, airy, blue and mysterious. On we went to *Par* for *Newquay*, *Truro* for *Falmouth*, to *Hayle* and at last to *St Erth* for *St Ives*. We got out, went over the bridge and boarded the little train.

We were going to Lelant, my own remembered place. Of course, the name had sound and colour – the sound of shelter and the colour of palest yellow but to me it meant a time of bliss as well and I longed to find out if it was still the same. Well, it was the same. Everything that I remembered was there – Station Hill, the rooks, the Cross, Church Lane, the clanking Kissing Gate, the Links, the Towans, the Beach and the Ferry. Tom Pomeroy, the ferryman, was still there and he remembered me and called me "Meery" as he always had done. Other people remembered me too and I hugged myself because it felt like home. Father went often to St. Ives by himself to take photographs, and said that when we got home he would make our bathroom into a darkroom so that he could develop the plates and make enlargements, and if I helped him he would buy me a camera. Of course, we went up to Tren Crom with a picnic basket and thermos flasks of tea and I climbed up to the highest point of the rocks to have the best view of the sea on both sides, and the sky seemed wider than I could ever remember. It was very much wider than in Birmingham and higher too but Birmingham is in England and Cornwall is not, so perhaps that made the difference.

There were some other differences which I didn't know about when I was living in Cornwall but now I noticed them. People in Birmingham used different words from what I could remember hearing in Lelant. Cornish children would call a wasp an *"Applebee"*, a woodlouse a *"Grammersow"* and say *"forth and back"* instead of "back to front", *"leave* me have a turn" instead of "let me have a turn" and "Mammy's going to put me to St Ives" instead of "take me to St Ives". They would never say "Our mom's on a line" if their mother was cross, but my friends in Harborne were always saying it, and "Caggy-handed" for left handed and "crabby" for bad tempered.

Of course, Cornish people couldn't be expected to know all the English words because English wasn't their very own language and they had been obliged to learn it, but their surnames were their own and they had some very nice Christian names too, like Morwenna and Loveday. I wished that I had a nicer name because *Mary Green* was so pale and washed out. I thought it made me sound as if I didn't count. Daddy made a kind of joke and said that we were called *Green* because

St. Ives Summer 1920

St. Ives Summer 1920

49

our forefathers were poor peasants who owned no land and therefore they had to take their cow to graze on the village green. If only they had not been landless I might have been called *Mary Meadows* and I rather liked the sound of it but I knew quite well that the only way to change my name would be to marry someone, some day.

As the days of our holiday hurried on, I was sure that although I should miss everything and everybody when we had to go home, most of all I should long for the sea – the sound of it, the colours and the everlasting graceful movement. It seemed to be saying something that I could not understand. It was like trying to recall a half forgotten dream.

When we were leaving I said, "Goodbye" to everybody but to myself I said, "I shall come back" and began to look forward to showing my friends at home my precious shells and a lucky stone and a dead crab. When I told mother that I wished that I was sunburnt like Tom Pomeroy she said that I would never get a rosy brown face like his because it was the salt water that made it so. I was determined to try, however and when we were at home once more I mixed some salt and water in a cup, painted my bare legs and arms and cheeks with it and climbed up to my favourite seat in the laburnum tree, facing the sun. It didn't really matter that I stayed as pale as I had always been because there were so many other things happening. School term started and there was a toy shop near to Scarf's grocery shop and I always had a quick look in the window as I passed on my way.

One Monday morning the toys in the window had been changed from what I had remembered being on show the week before, and there, high up, was the most beautiful big doll and I wanted it, to make clothes for it as if it had been my child. Mother said that I must wait for Christmas and that she would join the Christmas Club to pay for it. A week or two went by and I had to see it up there, every day. I longed to have it and was afraid that one day it would have gone, bought by someone else and although mother assured me that she had spoken for it to the shopkeeper, I could not be comforted and moaned so much that at last mother said, "All right, you can have it, but remember, it is your Christmas present from me," and we went straight away to pay the rest of the money and I carried it home very carefully lest her beautiful face got broken. As soon as possible I hurried to Miss Louie Warren's shop with my pocket money to buy some white wool, because there was a pattern for a doll's bonnet in my "Little Girl's

Fancy Work Book" and I made one but it wasn't quite big enough. I thought that by using a few more stitches and a few more rows of knitting it would turn out bigger so I carefully took a middle page out of my arithmetic book and marked the stitches in the squares, and when I knitted it and sewed it together, it was just right.

The big doll

I was soon able to work out more patterns and make some up for myself, and the doll looked very up to date and well dressed. Most of the mothers and aunts were knitting jumpers for themselves using the new "artificial silk" as it was called but I didn't like it because the garments were so droopy. Some toddlers were dressed in knitted woolly leggings and jumpers for outdoor wear, the little boys with caps and the little girls with bonnets. They looked like pixies and when I bought myself a baby doll and a little French doll from

Barnby's in the Great Western Arcade, I dressed them like that, and made clothes for indoors as well.

Dolls from Barnby's

It was more interesting to figure out the number of stitches to use for these little garments than the arithmetic I was having to do at school, like long division and fractions and I was very proud of myself when it came out right.

Before Christmas a very interesting thing happened. Father bought a boudoir grand piano from Sames' piano shop in New Street, and the house was full of music again, as it had been in Cornwall, when I was very small and danced when father played. I didn't dance now, but I tried to understand what the music was saying and could not but felt drawn to another world by it. One thing I did not really like, though. It was decided that I must learn to play this piano and so I began to have music lessons once a week with Miss Clark, who at first lived in the High Street and later moved to Lonsdale Road. Margaret had

Myself pretending to play the piano

lessons too, and although she was younger, she learned more quickly.

I tried hard and practised scales every day but I never progressed beyond Clementi's Sonatinas and was sure that however hard I practised I would never be able to play like my father did, and I was right. He played only the music of Chopin, Schumann and Liszt and I felt the excitement and mystery of it but when Mollie Jukes left the university and came to teach at the Clock Tower School in High Street in Harborne, she stayed with us for a while and played the music of Debussy and Ravel as well as the older classics and it was clear, even to a child like me, that their music was telling about another part of that other world. We were not always serious, however.

Sometimes father sang funny songs from the Gilbert and Sullivan operas and mother sang some jingles and bits of songs, like this:

"They call her Little Dolly Daydream,
Pride of Idaho, son now you know,
And when you go,
If something's on her mind,
Don't think it's you,
Cos no one's going to kiss that girl
But ME"

And this:

"Hello, hello!
Who's your lady friend?
Who's the little girlie by your side?
I've seen you with a girl or two,
Oh, oh, oh, I am surprised at you!"

And father sang:

"We'll all walk the wibbly, wobbly walk,
And all talk wibbly, wobbly talk,
All wear wibbly, wobbly ties,
And wink at all the pretty girls,
Wtih wibbly, wobbly eyes!"

Then there was, "Lily of Laguna" and "Tell me pretty maiden, any more at home like you?" And:

"Cora, Cora, captivating Cora,
She's the only lady I adore,
With a smila-ah, walking down the aisle-ah"

And so on and so on.

I didn't feel that I should grow up to be like these maidens and ladies – in the back of my mind I could hear a voice saying, "but not you".

There was: "Joshua, Joshua, Nicer than lemon squash you are," and "Lift me up a little bit higher, Obadiah, do," and "When I asked her if she loved me, she said, "What ho, not half! I love you for your whiskers Cos they tickle me and make me laugh," and I felt that I should always be too shy to join things like that. Father sang two ditties about girls that he called, "Blue Stockings" and one went like this:

"Maud, Maud, Maud,
The girl who has studied abroad.
Her father's new Steinway
Will be in a fine way,
The way it is hammered and clawed."

54

The other began, "Lydia, oh Lydia,
That encyclopedia,"

And I had the feeling that nobody really liked "Blue Stockings", because they were too clever, so I didn't want to be like them.

I liked wearing my best dress and going ot parties and dancing but mother sang this:

"With Varsovienne and gay Schottische,
She tickled my ear and gave a squeeze,
The County Ball is 'Go as you please' In Sligo!"

And this:

"Oh, it was beautiful,
Absolutely beautiful,
I never saw such a thing in all my life!
While the kids were having tea,
She was sitting on my knee,
And it was B-E-A-U-T-I-F-U-L!"

I had not been to parties like those and didn't really fancy them but this one sounded better:

"At our threepenny hop,
Our threepenny hop,
All the boys and girls are found,
Dancing round and round and round,
They won't go home 'til morning.
They never know when to stop.
It's 'Hi, Hi, go as you please.
At our threepenny hop!"

I could imagine myself there, as well as, "Up the ladder and down the wall" when the boys and girls came out to play in the moonlight, but "Not you" was what I could hear in my mind because I knew I should not be allowed to go. I did not seem to fit in anywhere. Boys had much more freedom and fun so I decided to be the next best thing, a tomboy, and do boyish things, like climbing trees and whistling. I knew a song about a boy who whistled, and it went like this:

"Day after day, I whistle in the gutter,"
(Then you had to whistle a few notes)
"To earn my bread, it never comes to butter"
(More notes).
"All day long I whistle round the houses,
Though I blow my best, the game don't pay,
'Cos I've holes in my coat and
patches on my trousers,"
(More notes to finish it off).

It was not always easy to sing and whistle, and keep to the tune and the rhythm but I tried.

Boys walked with a kind of swagger which I couldn't do very well and when they said "let's us go and have a swank" I knew that we girls were not welcome. In any case, dresses don't go with that kind of walking.

I liked my dresses much better than boys' clothes because theirs were made of tweed or serge and looked dreary, being mostly grey. I had by now grown too old for the "Rainbow" and "Tiger Tim's Weekly" and through the letterbox came "The Motor" and "The Autocar" for father, "Home Notes" and "Woman's Weekly" for mother and on Tuesdays, "Schoolgirl's Own" and on Thursdays, "The School Friend" for me. I had "The Children's Newspaper" and "Music and Youth" as well and father paid the bill for all these, and a daily newspaper too. I could hardly wait for Tuesdays and Thursdays to read about what fun and adventures those lucky girls had at boarding school and with my own pocket money I bought the weekly paper about the boys at Greyfriars boarding school, Bob Cherry and Billy Bunter and Hurree Jamset Ram Singh, the Nabob of Bhanipur because they seemed to have even more fun than the girls and they looked so nice too, in their long trousers and Eton jackets. I wished that I could know some boys like that and go to boarding school, but I knew that I never should because people from our *"walk of life"* just didn't.

I liked Hurree very much because he had a smiling brown face and spoke English in a funny way, and because he was Indian he was not so foreign as some other people were. This I knew because of "FID. DEF. IND. IMP." on pennies, standing for "Defender of the Faith" and

"Emperor of India" in Latin and as our king was the emperor, India was ours, in a way. Once the war was over and the Belgians went away, I don't think that any *foreigners* lived in Harborne but if there were any, my family did not know them. I was glad to be English because no one seemed to like foreigners very much and there were ditties which made them sound comical like this one:

"Oh, oh Antonio, he's gone away,
I'm all alonio, left on my ownio.
Oh, oh, Antonio, don't break my heart.
Come home, Antonio, with your ice-cream cart!"

And this one:

"Chin-chin Chinaman,
Muchee, muchee sad,
He aflaid, allee tlade
Velly, velly bad.
If no better soon,
Shuttee upee shop.
Chin-chin-Chinaman,
Hop, hop, hop!"

Obviously foreigners had misfortunes but not serious ones. In spite of speaking a kind of English, the Americans were quite foreign because some of their people were actually black, like the mammy of Epaminondas in "Home Notes". She was a little picture story, a cartoon, every week, and was a very black mammy in a very white dress, and was always telling her mischievous little piccaninny that he hadn't got the sense he was born with.

These black people lived in places with wonderful names – some white people sang little songs about them, like this one:

"Way home in Tennessee,
That's where I want to be."

They all sounded very nice people, sensible and happy and we sang about the Swanee river, and the steam trains running on the

57

Atchison, Topeka and the Santa Fe, and Margaret and I took parts in "Where d'ya work, ah John?" She sang the question and I sang, "On the Delaware-Lackewan," then she sang, "What d'ya do, ah John?" and so on until it was the end and I sang loudly and joyfully

"On the Delaware-Lackewan,
wan, the Delaware Lackewan."

It was all very jolly and when I sang:

"Hah-hee, ha-hee, he's waiting there for me.
I'll make him wait till half past eight,
Till white hairs grown on a black man's pate
Hah-hee, hah-hee, I'll make him wait for me,
Cos if anybody knows a thing or two,
It's me, me, me, me, me!"

I could visualise a beaming little old black man, proud of his white hair, but when I heard "Old Man River" and some of the negro spirituals, I began to wonder whether black people were as happy and quaint as we liked to think.

The year 1921 was rather different from the earlier years in several ways; instead of going on holiday to the seaside in the summer, we went to Malvern, once in April and once in October because it was father's turn not to have first or second choice of holiday. When we came home from Cornwall, father hunted in the Jewellery Quarter until he found a camera for me as he had promised. It was a tiny plate camera taking pictures two inches square. I am very proud of THE ABBEY GATEWAY because I took the photograph, and then helped to enlarge it when we came home. I must mot let pride overtake my story. A friend of ours had bought a cottage at North Malvern and allowed us to pay rent and stay there for short holidays as they did not live there but just went whenever they could, to enjoy the country air, and walk over the hills. We walked too, often to Great Malvern, where we had a meal at the Blue Bird Café before setting off to climb the Worcestershire Beacon, always by way of St Ann's Well, for a small drink of the special water, and to listen to the music, if we were there at the right time on the right day. This music was as special as the water, probably more so, because the water is still there and the music has gone. It was played by a blind musician who sat at a keyboard,

The Abbey Gateway, Great Malvern

but it was not a piano, or an organ, or a harmonium, but a Dulcitone, a dulcimer played by keys. It made a dainty sound of bells and the musician chose dainty tunes to play and I liked it very much.

If the weather was fine gypsies came with donkeys and one day it was decided that mother and I should ride up and that father should walk up and take some photographs of us on the way. When we reached the top and the gypsy had gone down, mother asked me if I had enjoyed it. I said that I had liked the donkey but that I didn't like the gypsy because she made rude noises, and mother could hardly stop giggling for long enough to say, "It was the donkey that did it, not the gypsy!" I felt sorry that I had thought wrongly about the gypsy but at least she did not know it.

When we went home after the October holiday, there began some serious talk about my going to a new school, because I was now too old to stay at Mrs Mac's any longer. The question for my parents was – where shall she go? Mother and I went to see the headmistress of Harborne College in St Peter's Road. It was a big house, and we were ushered into the drawing room and soon the headmistress joined us and said, "First of all, Mrs Green, I must ask whether your husband is in trade?" and when mother answered, "No", she said, "That's all right then," and asked a few questions about me and gave mother an

Riding up the Beacon

application form for my father to fill in and then we went home.

When Mrs Macready knew that I would be leaving her school at Christmas she gave me a letter to take home and it proved to be a very important letter, because in it she suggested that if I sat for the examination to go to King Edward's High School in New Street, I might pass it! There was a lot of talk about this idea between my parents and their friends and acquaintances. They had met a school master who had recently started a small school for boys in rooms in the big house in Queen's Park, and when he offered to give me some coaching, my father agreed. I went one day after school on the number 3 bus to the park and was met by the schoolmaster and taken in to the big room on the right of the hall.

It was very quiet because the boys had gone home and I felt shy and rather resentful because I had not wanted to have this coaching in the first place. However, he tried to make me feel welcome and when

I had taken my coat off he put his arm round me and said, "Now, come and sit on my knee and we'll do some arithmetic together." I was at once offended and demeaned, I had not sat on anyone's knee since I was a baby. I knew then that he and I were strangers for ever and very soon I said, "I think I had better be going now," and I hurried home. I told my parents that I didn't want to go again and when I explained why they said, "All right" and I felt pleased because I had not learned anything likely to help me in the entrance examination and when I sat for it, I passed without help from him. On the day of the exam, my parents met me and we went over to the Kardomah café for tea. Someone was coming out as we went in and when she saw the pencil case and ruler in my hand, she asked me if I had been taking the examination for King Edward's. I said, "Yes" and she then said, "I hope that you will be successful, because I went to that school myself." And she smiled very kindly and we all smiled back.

At that stage, the idea of going to a huge school every day, in the very middle of the city seemed unreal and I didn't think about it much because I had little confidence that I would "get in" but when I did "get in" and was offered a place and father agreed to accept it, I began to feel anxious about it all, especially when a list came, telling of all the items of uniform that I must have, and where they must be bought. My blazer must come from Hyams, with a gym tunic and blouses, and very expensive indoor shoes from Day's and a black velour hat and hat band from somewhere else. Mother didn't seem to approve of being told where to buy things because she liked to be careful with money but I was afraid of not looking right if my uniform did not come from the shops named on the list and I became across and miserable, and she bought the clothes and pursed her lips, saying that she could have made the blouses for less than half the price.

I had never worn a uniform before and when the day came for term to begin, I dressed myself in long black stockings, grey and white striped blouse, navy blue tunic, black blazer, dark grey coat and black hat, and felt very down-hearted and ugly. It was still as dark as night when father and I walker to Harborne station, and I thought that everyone in the carriage was staring at me and making fun because I looked so silly. When we left the train at New Street station people were rushing about in all directions and I wished that I wasn't there. It might have been easier if I had not been the only girl from Mrs Mac's but when father said, "Goodbye" and left me at that great door, I knew nobody, not one person, among all the crowd of girls hurrying to the cloakroom.

King Edward's Entrance Corridor and Porter's Lodge

The porter told us, the small group of obvious new girls, to wait, because a mistress would come to tell us where to go. Eventually, after changing my shoes and hanging my coat and hat in the cloakroom, which was like an enormous cellar, I was shepherded into the hall at the back for the ceremony of prayers. Miss Major sat on the stage in a chair like a throne and when she had read out one or two notices, someone played a march on the piano and we all filed out into the corridor, senior girls first. They didn't wear gym tunics like the rest of us, but were dressed in blouses and skirts, and loooked quite old, like grown up people.

When it was my turn to march out of the hall, one of the mistresses asked me my name and said that I was to be in Form Upper 3A, up the stairs. I found my way there with one or two other bewildered new girls and we were given a timetable each, and told what we must do, where we must go and what we must not do. I was worried to hear that I should have to play netball once a week because I didn't know how to play it, and the other girls did. We were taken to a room up the back staircase and given some exercise books and a pad with tear-off leaves and at eleven o'clock we were allowed to queue up in the hall for milk or cocoa in cups without saucers and I learned a new word, becaus they called this *"Recess"*. Back in the classroom, we were given a list of books which we had to buy at Cornish's across the street and told a few more rules, about *"Order Marks"* and *"Conduct Marks"* and that we

The School Hall

could go to Kent Street Swimming Baths on Tuesday afternoons and to Woodcock Street Baths on Thursday afternoons, because at those times there was clean water and only KE girls could go.

I had never been to a Swimming Bath and had never heard of either of those streets. My bobbed hair was tied neatly with new black moire ribbon and I thought that I looked quite nice but I was told not to wear the ribbon in future because it might catch fire in the laboratory during practical chemistry lessons. I felt that I should never fit in and I was glad to go home, and go to bed.

The next morning when mother came to light the gas in my bedroom and said cheerfully, "Time to get up" I said that I didn't feel very well. She said that I would feel better when I had washed and dressed and had my breakfast but I said that I couldn't eat anything and just wanted to stay in bed. Once daylight came I began to feel better and got up and dressed and had breakfast.

King Edward's High School, New Street

There was something else – the train had gone. I spent the day reading my Angela Brazil books which I had been given at Christmas. I felt guilty, a failure, miserable and ashamed. The bleak days went by and I admitted to no one that I was just suffering from fright but someone must have guessed, because I was not scolded. Dr Middleton came to see me and I was told that he suggested a new start at school, after half term. I knew that I should have to go some time, so I said, "All right" and reconciled myself to it. At least I knew where go to and some of the girls in my form smiled and asked me if I was better.

I soon learned that I was in a *form* and not a *class* and that Miss Ilse F Stearn was my *form mistress* and not my class *teacher*.

I tried hard to get used to everything, but for the rest of that term I longed for Fridays. After the Easter holidays I began to feel that I belonged to King Edward's, especially when I wore the blazer because it had 'KEHS" embroidered on the pocket in white silky thread and everybody could see it. Also, some rather interesting things began to happen, new for me, like the gymnastics lessons with "apparatus", in the boys' gymnasium, once a week in the afternoon.

It was fun to put hats and coats on and change into outdoor shoes, and walk, not *run*, along the pavement in front of the boys' school, down a narrow alley by Baynton's camera shop and into a small dark room in the school and there we hung our coats and changed back into our indoor shoes. It was not exactly dirty, that room, but it felt uncared for, like a box room without any boxes in it. I suppose we were kept away from where the boys were likely to be. I never saw one as we went along the narrow dark passage to the gymnasium. There the darkness ended. It was a wonderful place rather like a church, with windows high up on both sides. They were so high up that they had to be opened by a kind of corkscrew type of rod, turned by a handle down below. Once, and it was only once, we saw several faces looking down at us; some boys had crept out across the roof and were peeping and grinning. Our gym mistress, Miss Jaques, gave no sign that she had seen them, nor did we, partly because we were not supposed to tell tales, but they never came again so I think she did see them and had said a few words to the right person. Miss Ailsa M Jaques was a smiling person, but very strict, and we had to try hard to please her. She told us that when we knelt down our tunics must be six inches above the ground, hanging level all the way round and that we should press the pleats every weekend. My tunic was a "Standex" one, from Lewis's but now it was the summer term, and except for gym we could wear any dress provided that it was made of cotton material not silk. Austin's in Corporation Street sold lovely silk materials and when they held a sale, mother bought remnants at bargain prices, so I had silk dresses, but for school I had to have gingham or "print" ones with knickers to match.

Some more interesting things began to happen, and I was beginning to feel confident enough to join in. Miss Jaques offered swimming lessons at Woodcock Street baths once a week during the whole term and my father agreed for me to have lessons because I longed to swim and begged him to pay for them. Miss Jaques had a kind of strong fishing rod with a line and support dangling from it. I threaded my arms into the support and was floated across the shallow end of the bath several times, trying hard to move my arms and legs like a frog. I was eager and anxious. Suddenly she let the rod fall. I went under the water, quite frightened until she pulled me up and said sharply, "How can I teach you to swim if you don't do what I tell you to do?" I tried to say that with my new bathing cap covering my ears I had not heard what she said but her reply was, "Come along now, or your lessson will be over."

No. 4 Bus

I did learn to swim, but not in the Woodcock Street baths, because after being ducked I had no more lessons with Miss Jaques.

Our seaside holiday that year was two weeks at Teignmouth. I went into the sea every day and by the end of the holiday I was able to swim a few strokes without father's hand under my chin. I felt pleased with myself, and when we came home I went several times to Monument Road baths in Ladywood, the nearest one to Harborne, to practise and to show Miss Jaques next term that I was not as stupid as she seemed to think.

When my season ticket for the train was no longer valid, I began to travel to school by the number 4 bus. It cost fourpence for a return ticket, and I could board it at the top of Nursery Road and it took me to Warwick House in New Street, its terminus, before it turned for the return journey to Harborne. All I had to do was to cross the road and go into school, and at coming home time I didn't even have to do that, because it stopped right outside the boys' school which was next door to our school, built at right angles to it.

It was good to ride into town on the open top of the bus especially if it was a Daimler – the old Tilling – Stevens buses were rather shabby and rattled more. There was something very interesting being built at the bottom end of Broad Street, opposite to the Prince of Wales theatre – the new wireless studios for Birmingham. Father travelled to town on the train, as he always had done, with Percy Edgar who lived in Crosby Road. They were both interested in wireless tele-graphy but

66

for different reasons. Father learned all about how it worked and eventually designed and made a very fine receiver which took power from the mains instead of from accumulators, long before such equipment was available commercially. Percy Edgar was not so concerned about the technical side of it, but about what future there could be in it for people like himself, because "on the side" he was an entertainer. He ran a concert party called "The Greys" and sometimes they did their show on the wireless from a studio at Witton and then from an upstairs room at a picture house in New Street, and he realised the vast potential of the new medium for the Midlands, when the New Broad Street studios were in operation.

At the age of twelve years I felt that I was really much too old for Children's Hour wherever it came from but I could not help wondering whereabouts the uncles and aunties were, telling the serial story about furry animals called *Ambrose* and *Clatchy*. The Chad Valley toy factory in Harborne made Ambroses and Clatchies for sale and mother bought one, an Ambrose, I think, just for fun. One of the uncles often sang, "I'm looking for the Ogo-Pogo, the funny little Ogo-Pogo. His father was an earwig, his mother was a whale, I'm going to put a little bit of salt on his tail." It stayed in my mind but I thought it rather silly, being too old for it.

As my school was in the middle of town the governors thought that our school day should be from ten to nine in the morning until ten to one, so that we could be in fresh air in the afternoons but we had quite a lot of homework. I usually did mine before tea, or between tea and supper, because then I could listen in to something interesting before having to go to bed. There was the *News:* "Copyright by Reuter, Press Association, Exchange Telegraph and Central News" and after that there could be orchestral music, a funny man, like John Henry or Issy Bonn, Rawicz and Ladaner playing buets on two pianos, Flotsam and Jetsam singing, one doing all the high notes, the other all the low.

Clever people gave talks sometimes, but when Sir Oliver Lodge gave a series of talks on Friday evenings, what he talked about was too clever for me to understand any of it, but mother and I had to keep very quiet, while father listened to every word. Everybody liked the music programmes because there was every kind, whatever your taste. I had lived with music all my life, all of it, so called *serious* music.

There was father playing Chopin, Schumman and Liszt every day. I was taken to orchestral concerts in the Town Hall and on Sunday afternoons we three, mother, father and I walked to the university and listened to organ recitals in the main hall, and some of that music was very serious. Truly, I found Bach's Preludes and Fugues oppressive sometimes.

On the wireless there was a programme called "Composer of the Week", every evening and Christopher Stone introduced gramophone records, giving the details of each one after he had played it, so that people could go out and buy them if they liked. Miss Jaques used to take us for what she called "ten minute drill" on some days in the playroom and sometimes instead of swinging our arms around and doing "bunny jumps" and bending and stretching, she taught us folk dances and played the music on a gramophone. The records had been made for the English Folk Dance Society and we were invited to become associate members of it.

Main door of the High School

FROM THE PAST

200 YEARS AGO

The well-established inn known through three kingdoms as the Hen and Chickens in High Street, Birmingham, with stabling for about 70 horses, horse coach houses and other buildings will be sold.

Aris's Birmingham Gazette
November 1797

Backstaircase where the sign "Hen & Chickens" hung.

I did so, very eagerly, because I liked the dances much better than fox trots and one steps and the music was tuneful and elegant. One day, when I had stayed for a school dinner, I made my way to the door, expecting to step out into the street, but Miss Jaques was there and she waved me aside, because she was talking to a tall thin man in a Trilby hat, a dark shadow about to pass through the door into brilliant sunshine.

He shook her hand, raised his hat and went. She looked after him and turning to me, said, "Do you know who that was?" I shook my head and she said, "It was Cecil Sharp, and the work that he is doing will change your life." I couldn't see how so I just mumbled "Oh, thank you" and was glad to go. I felt quite grown up to go out into New Street alone, and look in the windows of favourite shops. Just across the road was Cornish's, the book shop where we bought our text books and we always felt welcome to go in and look at books, but at the beginning of term we were advised to go, on an appointed day, with our book list, to the "Second Hand Room" on the back staircase at school because if what we needed was there, it would be cheaper for father to buy. Although it was a room on what was called the Back Stairs, these stairs were, in fact, nearer to the front of the building than the main staircase, and on the wall at the top of the first flight hung the sign of the old coaching inn, the "Hen and Chickens".

Our school was built on the land where this inn used to be. I liked to look up at it and I felt rather proud of it because it was so old.

In 1923 several interesting things happened. We usually had a chemistry lesson one day a week, when we put on our chemistry overalls and went into the laboratory, where we mixed things in glass beakers, stood them on tripods over Bunsen Burners and wrote about what happened when the mixture warmed up – nothing much really, but it was a cheerful way to use up some time. However, one chemistry class in the SpringTerm was different. The mistress greeted us and said, "Today, we shall be doing some *Biology* so just sit down and take a few notes."

Behind her on the wall was a very large map of the inside of a person's body and with a long pointer she indicated the bones and the muscles, and then the different organs, and named them. This all took a long time, until we had made our notes, and it was almost the end of the lesson, and she said, "Then of course there are the reproductive organs, but that it all for now. Good morning", and walked rather stiffly out into the corridor. We all began to put our belongings into our cases, all except one laughing girl, who waved her notebook and said, "What a waste of time! She told us everything except the one thing we really want to know about!" Some nodded, some said, "Mmm", but I said nothing. I didn't want to talk about it because I didn't want to face the facts of growing up, that is the facts as I saw them. I occasionally looked up interesting words in the big dictionary, and sometimes the answer gave me another interesting word so I would look that up, and if that word made me even more curious, I would look for it in the *"Medical"* and *"Health"* chapters in Pears Cyclopedia. It was all rather cheerless, not something to look forward to.

I was reading romantic stories in magazines by Sapper, Saki, Dornford Yates, H. de Vere Stacpoole, books by Ian Hay and father now bought "Punch" and I read that too.

It all confirmed my belief that boys and men had much more fun

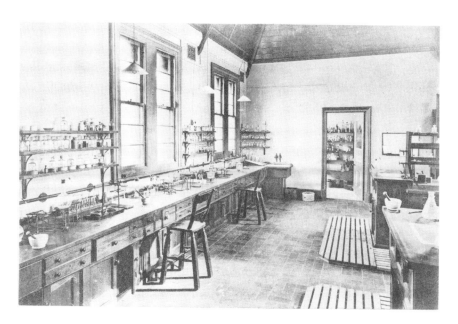

The Laboratory

and adventures than girls could ever hope to have. We girls at school must have known this, because a group of us decided to assume boys' names and not to answer to our own names. When one of my devoted aunts said kindly, "When you begin to "fill out', you'll have to think about choosing a corset or a corselette because of your figure." I told her quite rudely that I was *never* going to wear corsets, but I so disliked the idea of 'filling out' that with my pocket money I bought some wide ribbon and bound it tightly around my chest every morning and fastened it with safety pins. My aunt answered my rudeness rather sadly. "We *had* to wear corsets whether we liked it or not and we *had* to put our hair up whether we liked that or not, that is one thing you won't have to worry about, with your bobbed hair."

My mother was proud because she could nearly sit on her hair when she was a girl and she washed it with soft soap but I believed the advertisement in the magazines which said that "Friday night is Amami night" and bought "Henna for dark hair" while fair girls bought the camomile kind.

Looking back it surprises me that with all my striding about and boyish behaviour I still cared about my hair being shiny and my face having no spots, but I did care, and bought "Ponds Cold Cream" and

"Ponds Vanishing Cream" because according to advertisements in the magazines, "Society Ladies" used them and showed photographs of "Lady this" and "Lady that", all with perfect complexions because they used "Ponds Creams" on their faces.

In 1923 Harborne Swimming Baths were opened and we were all delighted. The rail at the shallow end had openings at intervals all the way along and out of them came crashing waves of water. Someone said that the bath water was drawn out at the deep end, purified somewhere underneath and pumped back at the shallow end to make the wave. It didn't smell like a wave of the sea but it was very exciting to hold the bar and let the water sparkle down, nevertheless. The changing cubicles were hinged to fold back against the wall and in the autumn a dance floor was laid over the empty bath, but in the springtime of the next year when swimming began again, there was no longer a wave at the shallow end because it was considered too dangerous.

Something very interesting happened at school that year – Miss Bull joined the staff. Some of our mistresses were quite old enough to be our mothers. I am thinking of the two Miss Ravenhills, Miss Cowell, Miss Makin, Miss Hooke – in fact, most of the staff, and they dressed rather like our mothers, too, except Miss Udall who always wore beautiful crepe-de-chine blouses, pastel coloured and with hand-embroidered collars. Miss Ward, Miss Baugh and Miss Whalley were even older, and all three reminded me of my grandmother, in their dark dresses down to their ankles and lacy collars up to their chins. So, there they were, and we respected them all, and then Miss Bull came!

She looked as young as any one of our sixth form girls. She had an Oxford degree in Classics, and her family actually lived there at Boar's Hill and she had played hockey for Oxford and she had been a pupil at Roedean School and her hair was shingled! It was a great and remarkable thing for us to have someone so modern on the staff. She began straightaway to pronounce Latin with hard "C's" and "W's" for "V's", and it made us feel very modern too and Latin and Greek became surprisingly popular! Miss Baugh had taught Latin before Miss Bull came and on entering the form room she would say politely, "Avete, puellae" and we said in a chorus, "Ave, domina!" and if we were too chatty she would say, "Tacete, puellae" and we cheerfully answered, "Tace, domina!" knowing quite well that we were being very rude in telling her to be quiet.

We would not have dared to behave like that during a lesson with Miss Bull, because she would have seen through the trick straight away. Sometimes we tried to ingratiate ourselves with a favourite mistress by bringing little posies of flowers to put on her desk, but Miss Bull showed very clearly that she was against that sort of thing – she left them where they were so the only way to please her was to do well in her Latin lessons, and I enjoyed it. To be honest, I really enjoyed school altogether now, and missed it in the holidays, because there was company and a lot of fun, although we were expected to work hard and do well in public examinations later on. I could sing in tune and was included in a small group of people from my house, Bordeaux, to compete with similar groups from the other three houses. I didn't always like the songs which were chosen for us, like "My love's an arbutus," and "Three little maids from school are we," and "Sir Eglamour, that valiant knight, who took up his sword and went forth to fight, with a fah, lah, lanky-down dilly". That one I thought rather silly but I liked to take part even so, because I was otherwise just a listener, not usually to songs. My home was full of the music of Chopin, Schumann and Liszt, all exciting and mysterious, but I also loved the dancing sounds made by banjos, guitars, mandolins and ukuleles, and to see the harpist beckon music from – "somewhere else", that other world. There wasn't time for much music in school because so much else was going on, like the Girl Guide company, the Debating Society and the "M.I.S." or Mutual Improvement Society, which was not as serious as it sounds, but a cheerful affair, especially as it met in the late afternoon and we had tea and cake as well as talk. Then people like me could go to an extra gymnastics lesson on Friday afternoons. I was no good at any games except cricket, and although some of us asked Miss Jaques very earnestly for cricket to be the summer game in the place of rounders, the answer was "No." When I began to play hockey, I was told to take my position on the wing and to stay out there so I did, and usually managed not to hit the ball at all. But I would have been happy to work on apparatus in the gymnasium every day of the week. I felt more confident in my gym tunic than in any other dresses and I pressed the pleats very carefully.

There was a lot going on in Birmingham and when we girls went to matinees at the Royal Theatre or the Prince of Wales in Broad Street, we went straight from school, wearing uniform, and no one took any notice of us, because we were always around in the city on weekdays.

When "The Valkyrie" came to the Prince of Wales Theatre in Broad Street, three of us decided to go to see it because it was the right thing to do, so after school dinner we hurried off and stood in King Edward's Place until doors opened for the evening performance. People kept coming to join the queue behind us and a fiddler and a juggler tried to entertain us by playing and doing funny antics and held out tins for a few pence. We took it in turns to walk up and down Broad Street and buy something to eat from Barrows at Five Ways and at last the queue began to shuffle along, round the corner into Broad Street, and inch by eager inch, to the Theatre box office where we bought our tickets for seats in the gallery. To reach this high place meant climbing up several flights of stone stairs and our seats were hard and cramped and in the very back row, but we were glad to sit down in them, nevertheless, and soon there was a quietness with everybody waiting, and then the storm of music began. I found it rather frightening.

By the time of the interval it had become very hot and stifling, so we left our seats and went to an open window at the top of the stairs and leaned out for a few deep breaths of fresh air and realised that the bar had opened its doors just behind where we had been sitting. It was full of people, mostly men, enjoying their drinks and talking cheerfully together. I said, "I'm very thirsty – let's have some lemonade", and I burrowed my way in, followed by my two friends.

The men made a little space for us and looked us up and down, and several raised their eyebrows and smiled at each other, but one asked me politely, "Did you want something?" and I said, "Yes, we want to buy some lemonade." He then said, "I think you will have to go back, because they can't serve young ladies like you in places like this", but when he saw our faces he said, "Go and wait in the corridor and I will bring you a glass of lemonade each, they don't mind me!" We tried to give him money to pay for the drinks but he said it was his pleasure. So we thanked him rather sheepishly and felt silly as we squeezed into our seats, wondering whether we should have refused to let a complete stranger treat us, but the interval came to an end, the safety curtain went slowly up and the bombardment of music began again.

When it all came to an end we were glad to go out into fresh air and say, "Goodbye". I made my way to the Number Four bus stop feeling almost stunned and was joined by a friend of my parents who asked me whatever I was doing there and when I told her where I had been, she looked at me with her head on one side and said, "Rather strong meat for you, I think." I mumbled something non-committal but the truth was that the meat was so much too strong for me that I have never since listened to anything composed by Wagner except by accident.

The School Library

There was a good library at school and we were encouraged to use it at recess, to choose and borrow books but we had to speak very quietly as the library was in two parts, divided by heavy curtains, and only people from the Upper School were allowed to use the inner part, when they had a free period, and could work or not as they pleased during that time. I was reading everything I could find and so it was easy for people to choose presents for me – books and books and books. Father bought the complete works of Dickens for my birthday, twenty volumes, and I read them all, one after another, not as a duty, but for the excitement of the stories and the people and their wonderful names, like "Mrs Slidaskew" and "Uncle Pumblechook" and "Lady Scadgers". I found these words as delightful as Lewis Carroll's "Frumious Bandersnatch" and the "Tulgey Wood" and the rest of

"Jabberwocky". It was pleasant to think of those two clever authors amusing themselves with their wordy inventions.

We girls often spoke to each other in an unusual way for fun. With matriculation the object, we now had to choose our subjects to study from groups determined by what was known to us as the "Northern Board" and the choice in one group was between "Greek, German and Geography". We had all learned Latin and French anyway and those like me who chose Greek or German used the first word that came to mind in any of those four languages, mixed with English, when speaking to each other. I'm sure we felt rather clever, showing off in this way, but in fact we were unaware of learning something very important about language and the English language in particular, without being taught. We were learning about "roots" by hearing words from other languages spoken in an understandable context. Our pronunciation was reasonably good, and I remember in my first term Miss Cowell asking us to bring a small mirror to our French lessons to learn *"Phonetics"*. She told us to watch her mouth when she made a French sound and then to make the same sound while looking in our mirrors and to pull the same funny face that she had done. It looked idiotic, but no one dared to laugh and at the end of that term we were no longer pronouncing French words and as we saw them on the printed page. We began to feel the sound of words, to connect the separate sounds with their meanings, with no thought of grammar.

My Granny Schofield knew a lot of very interesting words which were not in my dictionary and my mother could remember even more, "Pottery talk" she called it and often laughed when she used words and phrases which reminded her of childhood games, and happy times with her sisters. She said that they played "Dobby off my Cob" and it seemed to me that when I was a little girl we played something like that, called "I'm the King of the Castle" and what we called a "Seesaw" they called a "Queedle". If I was slow, she sometimes said, "Look slippy" and spoke of mischievous boys as "Rumty-fizzers" but if they were rather naughty she called them "Rappertags" and when they ran away she said, "they tibbied off". I never heard people in Birmingham using words like "strug" for a stray cat or dog, and "motty" for a promise or "blart" for crying with noisy tears or any of the other North Staffordshire words which mother could use if she wanted to and I was glad that she only said such words at home because people might think that she didn't know any better if she used them all the time, but it was interesting.

In winter time she would often say, "It's as cold as *Okey* today" or "I'm as cold as *Okey Pokey*" and when I asked her why she used those words, she said that she didn't really know, but father said that when the Italian ice cream men were in town with their little handcarts they would shout "Ecce Poco, penny a slice, all very sweet and all very nice!" and that *"Ecce Poco"* became *"Okey Pokey"* meaning "cold as ice".

I was beginning to enjoy words very much, no matter whether they were slang or dialect, or foreign to English. I really looked forward to French and Latin and German lessons because of the enlightenment they gave. For instance, when I had first heard, "Somer is icumen in, sing cuckoo" I thought that it meant, "Summer is a coming in" but when I heard "-ist gekommen" in my German lesson I was sure that the song meant that summer had come and that when my Granny said, "Is your mother come'n in?" with the "n" sound quite clear, she was speaking a very old kind of English indeed. It was a pleasure to talk with her and ask questions and I found out that when she was a girl she wore a crinoline but not for long because the fashion changed. She used to wear pattens when she mopped the paved part of her garden and explained that she would then "Trindle the mop, like this" and showed me how she rolled the handle of the mop up and down her out-stretched left arm quickly, to spin the water out. She enjoyed telling me these things and it gave me a glimpse of the past in my mind's eye whenever I went to stay with her and Auntie Mary for a few days during school holidays but I did not go there at Easter, 1925.

One day, in the school library Nancy Mauger whispered "Have you read this?" and showed me a book called "The Abbey Girls go back to school." I hadn't read it so she told me that when some of the girls in the story had just left school, they went to London for a week to learn Folk Dancing and Morris and Sword Dancing! It sounded like perfect heaven and we decided there and then that as soon as we were old enough, we would go to one of these Holiday Schools and stay in lodgings and attend classes at *Chelsea College of Physical Education* – it all sounded like an exciting adventure. But it didn't happen. Nancy's father accepted a new job as manager of a long stretch of railway and he was pleased because it was an important and very well-paid job but – it was to take care of the whole of the rail track from Dublin to Cork in Ireland! So the family had to move from Solihull to Dalkey and I missed Nancy very much. But – after Christmas *she* wrote to *me* and *her* parents wrote to *my* parents, with an invitation to go and stay with them for the Easter holidays! Father said, "Of course, you must go" and he and Nancy's father made all the arrangements for the journey, and mother bought me a new Spring coat from Mrs Kilby and made me a new dress of Viyella material to wear with it, but Nancy had written to say, "You must bring your gym tunic," so I packed that and blouses and black Sylkestia stockings and navy blue knickers, very short and tight. I was rather pleased with myself in my gym clothes and I hoped that we should be wearing them most of the time. They made me feel sure of myself.

It seemed a long time to wait for the end of term, but it came at last and then, very soon, it was *the day!* Father travelled with me to Crewe, where it was arranged that we should meet Nancy's father, who would take me the rest of the journey. He had already been to Wolverhampton to collect two other girls of my age, daughters of friends, but not of the same family. They didn't know each other until today and I didn't know them, so Mr Mauger and father had to do all the talking until our train came in and four of us boarded it, and puffed away, waving "Goodbye" to father, standing by himself on the platform. I think that we girls were all rather scared of having to go by boat to the place called "Kingstown" on my map, and it proved to be for me a very unpleasant experience, not because I was seasick but because I wasn't. Nancy's father had booked bunks for us and as soon as we were on board he handed us over to a stewardess, who took us down and showed us which bunk each one must climb into. It was very gloomy and I am sure that by the time we moored up at Kingstown I was the only person down there who had not been sick, and I felt as pale and forlorn as those who had. We were glad to be bundled into a taxicab, but not nearly so glad as we were to tumble out of it and see Nancy and her mother and her brother Peter beaming at us from the doorstep of their house.

So it began, and by breakfast time the next day we were all beaming, although still a little shyly, but soon it was my delight to be part of a big family, five children all taking turns to clear the table, wash up, dry up, put away or lay the table again but I let one of the others lay the first place, in case I betrayed ignorance – they seemed to use more knives and forks than we did at home; however I soon remembered the order and laid everything in its proper place and was happy. The weather was sunny and breezy and Nancy said, "Let's go down to Killiney beach and do some gymnastics," so we put on our tunics and blouses and took off our stockings and away we went, chattering about nothing but the fun of it all. As we turned a high corner, before running down to the beach, we met a tall grey-haired priest wearing a black soutane. I was very surprised because at home our vicars and parsons only wore their cassocks in church. He stood still, looking at us from top to toe and back again and it was clear from his face that he did not like us at all. He seemed quite shocked – I was dismayed because I didn't think that we had done anything wrong, but we walked quietly past and he watched us until we were out of sight, when we felt free to run cheerily down to the beach. The tide had left the sand gold and firm and we couldn't wait to show off our cartwheels and handstands to each other. We tied our girdles very tight but when we were upside-down, our tunics came over our eyes so we took them off and put them in a neat pile and Nancy's brother looked after them. He was nine years old and not at all interested in doing cartwheels. The priest was not there so he could not be even more shocked. In fact there was no one else there at all. It felt very, very good to be so free, and whenever we had nothing else to do, we were there and the sun seemed to shine all the time.

However, Nancy's parents arranged some very nice treats for us. One day we took a picnic to Bray Head and rode on a very narrow railway and another day we went to a small river called the Dargle and were driven up a lane to a place on the river bank, in a Jaunting Car, and when I was told about it, on the day before, I thought we should be going in an open motor car called a *Jaunting Car* because people hired it to go for a jaunt in, but it wasn't a motor car at all. It was a high cart, drawn by a horse and two people faced forward, like the driver, and two people faced backward, on seats made of planks. We four girls climbed up, and Peter sat dangling his legs at the back and the driver seemed to like us very much, waving his hat and his whip and telling us not to be afraid because he would do his best not to tip us out on to the road, and we all giggled and squealed at every jolt. It was a most joyful ride and when we reached our picnic place, we all jumped down and the driver took the cart back to pick up Nancy's parents.

The stream was shallow and we hopped from stone to stone as it curled around them and sparkled gently. I am surprised that a day on which I did little is even now so clear and full of wonder in my mind. Of course, I had never ridden in a Jaunting Car before, and have never done so since. That must be why. It's a "Once upon a time" and "happy ever after" kind of day. We were all invited to a Dinner and Dance one evening at a hotel in Kingstown but Nancy said that we must never say that name because people didn't like it any more and we must call it by its Irish name of Dun Laoghaire, and she told us how to say it. I wore my home-made party dress of peach coloured crepe-de-chine and felt rather awkward at a grown-ups party, in case I looked like an overgrown child, but we younger people were seated together at dinner and danced together when the music began so I was one of a group and not one alone, and could sidle to the back of the others, putting on a smile so that if anyone looked at me, it would seem that I was having a lovely time. If only the dancing was Folk Dancing I might have had a really lovely time because I had heard some Irish music now and again and it seemed the kind of music that you had to laugh and dance with, but the dancing here in the ballroom was very sober and no one seemed to be enjoying it much, but we had fun between ourselves and went home earlier than anyone else because we were young. The dinner was very nice with a pudding called a "Bombe Glace", quite new to me.

One day we spent in Dublin, partly because everybody who goes to Ireland must see Dublin, Nancy said and partly because the holiday was nearly over and we wanted to buy some little presents to take home for our parents. Mrs Mauger took us to see a place where she said that "the troubles" had begun. This place had been a Post Office in "Sackville" Street but now it was a ruin in "O'Connell" Street. I knew nothing about any troubles and asked no questions, not wanting to show such ignorance, but I thought about it. When we all got tired of walking round the streets, we sat on the steps of a big church to rest and watch the river Liffey. It was a rather dull day and the river was very dull, almost mud coloured but I found it strange and interesting to see persons going in and out of the church, all the time, in and out, dipping their fingers in a stone bowl, crossing themselves and bowing and curtseying. I had never seen anything like it.

Our last picnic was at a park called *Phoenix* and the Irish parliament house was there, looking lonely in the greensward. Next day, we played our last Demon Patience after our last high tea, packed our cases, said our last "Goodnights" and the next morning began our journey home, with much waving and blowing of kisses. At the boat I would not go down into the darkness and lie on a bunk, but sat on

deck all the way, with Mr Mauger and stared at the flat, grey sea and the low, grey sky, sulking together in ominous stillness. I began to think about home. The more I thought, the slower the journey, but at last, we all came ashore, boarded our train, and at long last I was seeing my daddy on Crewe station, in his raincoat and Trilby hat, looking for me. On the journey to Birmingham I talked all the time and then when we got to Tudor Cottage and I saw mother I said it all again.

She was quite interested but seemed rather keen that I should go to my bedroom and unpack and eventually I did so and understood why. In my absence, she and father had gone off to *Golby's* in the village and bought me a new bed, new curtains and a lovely rug for the bedroom floor. I was really pleased and glad to be at home again. Mother was always pleased when I was happy, but I was so full of myself that I asked straightaway for a bedside lamp and a new dressing gown.

I did not realise then, what a dainty person mother was. She liked to make blouses of fine material with lace and she knew the names of the lace she used – Torchon and Valenciennes and so on, but to me it was all just lace. She liked tiny things, so it was easy to buy presents for her and if father came across any little objects, like the cookery book and the stamp purse, he would buy them for her, to keep with the Rubayat of Omar Khayyam which he had given to her when they were first acquainted.

Mother's Little Things

It was a temptation to me to look in the window of Jay Viggars' shop opposite to school in New Street and I spent a lot of spare pocket money on objects offered for show there, because I also liked small things. I bought a very neat cabinet from Corbett's in Harborne High Street to keep my collection in and found it a bargain for only four shillings and sixpence.

My Cabinet and Things

Apart from the books mother carried some of her little things in her handbag, because they were useful, and that was where she and I differed because my things were all like miniature toys. It may be that they enabled me to feel like a child without appearing babyish because although I could not avoid getting older, I did not look forward to becoming a "Grown-up". However, when mother bought for herself the book of the Queen's Doll House, we were both enchanted by it.

When the Autumn term began school started to prepare us for Matriculation because we should be sitting the examination in two years time and if we did not at least achieve a School Certificate, we "stayed down" until we did so or left altogether. We had new weekly timetables to fill in, to show how much time we spent in homework on

The Queen's Doll'sHouse

each subject each day, at what time we went to bed, and a parent or guardian was required to sign them. I don't think we felt oppressed at all, we were expected to do well and knew it without being told, so most of us worked fairly hard but still had plenty of fun.

Some of it was rather silly, like the time the whole form agreed that each one of us would come to school with our hair cut in a fringe. We thought that our form mistress would be very surprised at the change in our appearance, but she took no notice at all and we decided that she had no sense of humour. We often did little plays, sometimes just reading them, but when we heard the depressing news that Miss Major was leaving, because she was going to be Head of Girton College, we heard the exciting news that Sir William Orpen was going to paint a portrait of her, to hang in the school hall, and that we, the school, would put on a great play for her and her friends to say "Goodbye" in a memorable way.

Miss E H Major

This play was a dramatised version of Mark Twain's story, "The Prince and the Pauper", very suitable for us to do because this "Prince" in real life became our "King Edward the Sixth" and the last act of the play was rewritten, presuming to explain how it came about that he founded the school. I had a part in this play, and made my own Tudor-style costume to wear in it. It was a speaking part but all I had to say was "Largesse, largesse!" over and over again in a crowd scene so I could not possibly forget my lines! It was a very exciting play for the whole school, especially when our parents came to see it and I think we were all sorry when it was over. It was very hard for Miss Barrie

to feel at home when she came to be our head mistress because we had all loved Miss Major so much. But we got used to the new ways in time and found much to enjoy, both in school and everywhere else.

Miss Barrie

Each autumn, the swimming baths in Harborne were emptied, cubicles folded back to the walls and a very shiny wooden dance floor laid down. Margaret and I began to go to the dances from time to time, to meet friends, mostly girls, but some boys began to come and they usually stayed together and we girls danced with each other, because the boys didn't dance as well as we did, but we drank lemonade and chatted and giggled with them. It was not a very charming place to meet in because the lighting was very bright, all right for when it was a swimming bath but cold for a dance hall, the glass roof was too high and the walls were tiled so that the sound came back hard and unfriendly, but there wasn't anywhere else in Harborne except the Moorpool Hall and that hall was often used for plays.

Margaret and I wore our "best" dresses but I would not wear high heeled shoes, because I thought they made women walk in a stilted way and spoiled the shape of their legs by tilting them on to their toes.

I didn't like dresses that hung straight from the shoulders as the fashion was at that time, so that when our mothers decided it was time to have ready-made party frock instead of home-made ones, I was worried in case I might have to wear something without any sign of a waist and with no swinging fullness, but Margaret and I talked it over and decided that we would not agree to have any dresses if we didn't like them. So we went with our mothers to Keith Pilley's dress shop in the village and spent a whole afternoon, probably a Saturday, trying on and at last I found one that I liked.

It was made of peach coloured georgette, with a lace yoke, sleeveless, as was the fashion then and, although the waist was a little lower than my real waist, it was there that the very full skirt joined the bodice and it twirled beautifully because it was made partly of the same silk lace as the yoke, and that gave it weight. I rather fancied myself in it. However much I did not want to grow up, I had to admit that it was beginning to happen, and that I must make the best of it, but it wasn't easy. I wanted to be a modern girl, but not a "Bright Young Thing", like those in the Punch cartoons, so I decided what I would not do, hoping to turn out likeable.

I would not wear high-heeled shoes, or strings of beads, or corsets or smoke cigarettes in long holders or even wear those awful Russian boots which were very fashionable but very ugly and saggy round the ankles. I wanted to feel good and be liked by people who thought I looked good, so when it came to the end of the Autumn term I really looked forward to wearing my new dress at the school Christmas party. This was an unusual party because there was music to dance to but no one danced until the very end when we all squeezed into the

hall and danced, "Sir Roger de Coverley" with much bumping and laughter. A week or two before the date of the party, we provided ourselves with little dance programmes, pink or pale blue, printed in silver or gold, with a tiny pencil on a ribbon and more ribbon to make a loop for one's wrist. Inside there were spaces so that names could be written in for each numbered dance, and anyone could book a dance with anyone, even with a mistress if she was agreeable and the so called dance was an arm-in-arm walk anywhere in school, even in the cellar, talking and talking and most of us visited the skeleton who was allowed to dangle outside his cupboard for this evening so that we could shake his hand.

Looking back, as I now must, it seems a very dull event to be called a party, but it was exciting to talk to mistresses about clothes and holidays and cosmetics, as if they were just ordinary friends and not people to be obeyed. Several of my form-mates said, in passing, "Like your dress", so I went home feeling pleased with myself and looking forward to Christmas. I had several invitations to parties in the New Year and I always enjoyed going to Margaret Adams' party in Acocks Green because she belonged to a family of five and it was a pleasure for me to be one of a crowd instead of one alone. However, one morning there was a knock on the door, and I opened it to see Margaret and two of our friends standing there laughing. She said, "We have got to visit all the guests to tell them our party is off, because my brother George has got the measles!" It was disappointing but at least there were one or two other parties and my parents and I were going to the Prince of Wales theatre in Broad Street to see "No, No, Nanette" with the Hewitt family for a Christmas treat and it felt that this would be a special occasion, because our seats were in the *Dress Circle*.

The day before we were to go, I developed a streaming cold but I was determined to go, although my eyes watered so badly that I could hardly see the stage. The next day I felt quite poorly and stayed in bed. The next day I felt really poorly and mother sent for Doctor Middleton who asked a few questions and then said to mother, "She's got the measles. Draw the curtains and keep her up here until the spots have come and gone". I felt quite hard done by to have such a childish illness when I was nearly seventeen and very gloomy because I couldn't see well enough to read, so I asked father to buy a tin whistle for me and I tried to play folk dance tunes.

I had heard someone playing folk tunes on the traditional *"Pipe and Tabor"* and hoped to do the same one day, but anyone hearing the sounds which I was making would not have felt very confident in my success. I looked so ugly that I wondered whether I should ever recover my own face again but I did and after three weeks, I went off happily to school, looking forward to telling my friends about it, but on the way something unusual happened and I had to tell them about that instead.

Number Four buses at that time went round the town in a loop, not always the same way round. If it said, "Via New Street" on the front, the bus went from the Town Hall down New Street, up Corporation Street, round into Colmore Row to the Town Hall and back to Harborne but if it said "Via Colmore Row" it went the opposite way. On this, my first day back at school, my bus was a Colmore Row one, so I decided to get off at the Town Hall and walk down New Street. I had not gone far when I realised that someone had caught up with me. It was a new young mistress who had not been at school long and did not take any of my classes, so it surprised me when she said, "Hello, Mary. It's nice to see that you are back at school. Have you been ill?" I told her that I had caught measles at the school party and she said, "What a pity. You looked so sweet in your pretty dress," and gave me a winning smile.

Such a remark was to me so shocking that all I could say was, "Oh." It was a very flat kind of "Oh", but it was full of meaning, saying, "Go away. Leave me alone. Mistresses don't say things like that to their pupils. I don't like it. Go away." But she didn't go away and I had to walk with her beside me all down New Street until we went into school, when I said, "Excuse me," and ran downstairs to the cloakroom. I couldn't wait to tell someone of my odd encounter and soon I had a small group of form-mates muttering around me. One of them, a very dancing girl called Betty, said that the mistress concerned had asked her a question in class about something or other, and when she replied, began to cry and ran into the corridor and didn't come back. In fact, she never came back to school at all and we were told that she had left because she had been taken ill.

We whispered about it and wondered. One said, "She didn't look ill" and another said, "Perhaps she had a nervous breakdown, or something," and then we forgot about it because there were so many other interesting things to talk about, like the General Strike, for instance.

This happened in 1926 and I, for one, had no real idea about the misery and distress that caused it. The daughter of a colleague of father's was to be married in Wylde Green and we, the Greens, were invited. Mother and I had new dresses and new Spring coats to wear with them, and new dainty hats, and we were really looking forward to this wedding but we never went to it because we couldn't get there. The strike happened, and there were no trains and no buses and it was very unlikely that anyone would risk driving a taxi or car.

I never heard whether anyone apart from us was prevented from going to the wedding but I was determined to get to school somehow on the following Monday so I got up early and started to walk. As I went down Harborne Hill a bus passed, driven rather quickly by a beaming young man and alongside him on the bonnet of the bus sat someone hugging a rifle in his arms.

When at last I got to school, I was rather late and could not wait to tell someone about the men on the bus because it was exciting. One of my friends said that they must have been students from the university, her brother had volunteered to do the same although it was very dangerous because the strikers were going to wreck the buses. Then another girl chipped in and said that her brother had driven a train to London and that he was afraid of not finding out how to stop it before he ran into the buffers at Euston and we all laughed, because she told it as if it was a funny story, knowing that her brother had managed it all perfectly well and had driven another train back to Birmingham. Apparently, he made a joke, saying that he had always wanted to be an engine driver!

The next day I left home earlier and tried to walk faster than I had done before, because those of us who managed to get to school were greeted with nods and smiles of approval, and I liked that. When I reached the top of Chad Hill, a taxi cab pulled into the kerb. It was definitely a taxi cab but the driver was not a taxi man, he was another of those beaming students and he shouted to me, "Going into town?" "Yes", I said, "New Street?" he said. I said, "Yes" again. "Get in and be quick," he said, so I tried but I was pulled in and squeezed by somebody very tightly or the door would not have shut and we sped away, letting someone get out at Five Ways. As there were no traffic lights in those days and no traffic on that day, we went very quickly, so I was at school much earlier than I really wanted to be, but it was fun.

As the days went by, vehicles of every kind began to come back on to the roads, and life gradually returned to what it had been before the strike began, but not for the miners. They ended with even less wages than they had before and were in great misery but we girls knew little about that side of it because Birmingham was not a mining area. I thought of them as "those poor people" sorry for them and glad not to be poor too, although my family was not well off like the people I was reading about in the monthly magazines. They ate their dinners in the evening whereas we all had dinner at midday and supper in the evening or "high" tea which was rather more savoury than the usual tea of bread and butter and cake but if we had "high" tea we did not have supper as well but may be a milky drink just before bedtime. The wealthy ones in my magazines had a fairly light meal at midday and called it "lunch" but if my family's friends had "lunch" it was a mid-morning drink of tea or cocoa with a biscuit, or on special occasions, a glass of wine and a small piece of fruit cake. I thought that the well off people were very stiff and had little fun in their lives, so I did not want to be like them, but I wanted to know all about them and that was easy because all the stories were about the well off and not about the poor.

We just knew that some people were so poor that they begged for money in the street and that some people were not quite so poor but the wives took in washing or went out as charwomen because the men in the family earned low wages. It did not worry me very much because I was so concerned about myself and what I should be and do when I left school.

After passing the matriculation exam I really had to think about what I should do next. One of the mistresses said, "You have chosen the order of subjects quite wrongly. It should have been French and German as main subjects and Latin as the subsidiary one. You will find it very unlikely to get a teaching job the way things are." I did not like to say that I did not want to be a teacher anyway. When father asked me if I had any idea of what I would like to do, I said that I would like to tell stories on the wireless like A J Alan. He made up stories and told them as if they were true, and mother and I really looked forward to listening to him, but when a group of us girls were discussing what we would like to be, I said that I would like to get married and a have a family of children.

I sent away for a prospectus of what was then called *"Remedial Drill"* because it was a kind of gymnastics planned to help people to

90

delight in movement, and I was sure that I would be quite good at it, but when I saw how high the *fees* were, I didn't think it was fair to expect father to pay so much money and I threw the prospectus away before he even saw it. I tried not to worry about it because life could be fun, especially now, with no examinations looming over me. There were some amusing jokes which became "the done thing" from time to time, often said to be lucky, like making sure that your first word on the first day of the month was "Rabbits" and shouting "Beaver" if you saw a man with a beard and "King Beaver" if his whiskers were of a ginger colour. In the upper school somehow a small rule became known and unless you obeyed it and wore a coloured silk handkerchief in your blazer pocket, you simply did not count. While the craze lasted we gave them to each other for birthday and Christmas presents, and wore them very proudly. Then suddenly no one wore them any more.

There was one thing to ensure good luck that everyone did, we all "touched wood" or pretended to, and just said, *"touch wood"*, meaning *"I hope so"*. But a new style of doll came on the market, a small standing up doll with a pixie face and its two thumbs very firmly "up". Because its face looked like Cupid it was called a "Kewpie" doll and because of its thumbs it was called the "Fums Up" doll and it was the very best thing to have if you wanted good luck. That is what the advertisements said, any way. Then someone had a wonderful idea, and began to manufacture these little creatures, tiny, like charms, to wear on a necklace or chain, but each one had its head made of *wood* and they were called *Tiki Touchwoods*.

Anything small appealed to me, so I bought a rather cheap one, but I was given a very nice silver one, and although I don't think it has brought me much luck, I am rather fond of it.

At school I and my form mates were now Big Girls and we walked about and even sometimes, stalked about, in what seemed to us a properly dignified manner and we went, in twos or threes, to matinees at theatres and cinemas if we felt that we ought to go to a

Fums up Tiki

particular show. When I saw that Pavlova would be dancing in Birmingham I was determined to see her because she was famous and this was to be her last tour, so two or three of us went to the Prince of Wales theatre and sat in the "Gods". We were told that she was not going to perform all the dancing billed on the programme because she was tired and needed to save her strength for the *Dying Swan* which she did, and conveyed a great sadness, as the supposed bird drooped and died, perhaps because she herself was to droop and die before long.

Behind the Prince of Wales theatre in Broad Street was the Bingley Hall and when the *Trades Exhibition* took place, that is where it was held. Some of the trades people showed goods and processes, using dutiable materials and as an Excise Officer, my father had to go and observe and was issued with a free ticket to admit him and "one other" and that "one other" was often *me*. It was very entertaining with so many stands fitted up to show how different things were made, and especially good in the evenings, when military bands played, a different band each week. Of all the visits I made to this exhibition, which took place every year and lasted several weeks, one in particular I could never forget, because the star attraction was the famous *Fairy Fountain.* It was set in the middle of the hall and people gathered round it in increasing crowds as every evening the time came for it to begin to play. The band played dainty music to match the sequence of sparkling water as it rose and fell back, then rose higher and fell again until it reached the very ceiling of that high building, bathed all the time in gently moving pastel light. It was a really lovely sight, so enormous, yet filigree all the way, and dancing.

Everyone went to cinema for reasonably priced entertainment and the "West End" in Suffolk Street was quite the smartest in town, so we girls could have dinner at school and walk up there to see anything we fancied. At one time the management set out tables and chairs at the back of the auditorium and viewers could have afternoon tea and watch some of the picture at the same time, so of course we had to try out this new thing, but we were not very enthusiastic, because for the film to show up, lighting had to be dim, and then you couldn't see which little cake to choose. The experiment was soon abandoned so I think that other people must have felt as we did and not taken tea there again.

Although we were now big, in any activity even remotely

connected with school, we were still school girls, but when I went anywhere with my parents, I had to try to appear grown up. On fine Saturdays in the summer, I went to the *Harborne Cricket Field* with them and had done so for years, but I no longer played ball and ran about when the teams were having tea. I sat quietly on a plank seat and when they played, I watched them, and tried to make intelligent comments now and then. Someone made very nice little cakes and scones which we could buy unless the teams ate more than expected at their tea time. It was all rather sedate and English, to watch village cricket, but there was one thing at that pavilion which made the whole place feel unusually countrified; it had an Earth Closet, the only one I had ever seen. It was very small, tucked in behind a wooden door, marked "Ladies Only" in small letters. Behind the door was another door and behind that door was the closet, with a wooden seat across the back. The middle part of this seat depressed an inch or two when it was sat upon and sprang back up when the person stood and then about a bucketful of fine grit slid into the cavity below. This grit smelled strongly of Jeyes Fluid and it was such an interesting process that when I was a little girl, I and my friends often "went" without real need, just to make it happen. Now that I had to watch the cricket, I began to take more interest in Harborne Second Eleven than the First Eleven because several of the Second Eleven players were quite young and I though how pleasant it would be if one of them would notice me and look twice and maybe smile, but no one ever did, and I felt that I was a nobody, that I didn't count or fit it anywhere. However, something interesting happened.

Father retired, and announced that he was going to buy a motor car. He knew a lot about them, and set off one day by himself to choose one at a motor car show room in the city, where he paid the price asked for a Morris Oxford Saloon, got in the driving seat and drove home. It took rather a long time because he had never driven a car before and mother and I were relieved and excited when he drew up outside the house. He took it out every day for a week or two before taking me for a ride and then said one evening, in a rather thoughtful way, "Mother and I have been thinking that when you have left school in the summer, it would be a pleasant change if we let this house furnished and rented a cottage in the country, perhaps Malvern, to see how we like a quiet life away from the city. What do you think?"

It was such a new idea that I had to ponder before nodding my head. I felt little confidence in the future. And then I had a brilliant idea. "Let's go back to Cornwall. That's where we belong." Father said, "Well, we shall have to see." Mother said nothing, but smiled because I was smiling. So, plans were made. Our house was to be let, a cottage was to be rented in Lelant, and these arrangements took much time and fretful work, to which I contributed no help whatever. I was living in a dream of excitement and disbelief, longing to go, but fearful sometimes. However, at last with all done, we went.

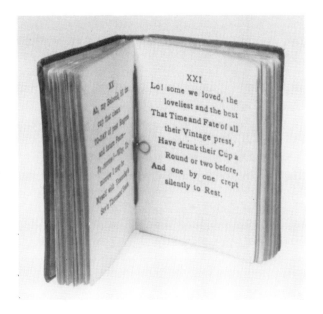